A NARRATIVE OF ETHAN ALLEN'S CAPTIVITY

Containing His Voyages & Travels

ETHAN ALLEN

With an Introductory Note by John Pell
Illustrations by Will Crawford

Dover Publications, Inc.
Mineola, New York

Bibliographical Note

This Dover edition, first published in 2013, is an unabridged republication of the edition printed in 1930 for The Fort Ticonderoga Museum by Richard W. Ellis; The Georgian Press, New York.

International Standard Book Number
ISBN-13: 978-0-486-49101-1
ISBN-10: 0-486-49101-3

Manufactured in the United States by Courier Corporation
49101301
www.doverpublications.com

CONTENTS

ILLUSTRATIONS

Introductory Note

by John Pell, *Esqre*

✤✤✤✤ THAN ALLEN, it is commonly
✤ E ✤ supposed, was a pioneer, backwoods
✤✤✤✤ chieftain and extempore soldier who
suddenly emerged from the wilderness at
the head of a band of uncouth adventurers,
captured a fortress, shouted an epigram and
disappeared again into the obscurity of
mountain caverns and first growth trees.
Like so many successful military leaders who
have become semi-legendary heroes, his life
is remembered as a single incident and a few
words,—the capture of Ticonderoga "In the
Name of the Great Jehovah and the Continental Congress". The consequences of this
event were indeed far reaching. As the first

aggressive military action of the colonists it converted the armed resistance of a few Massachusetts radicals into a war for independence. Further, it was the British guns from Ticonderoga which drove the British troops from Boston. But in a life of fifty-two years the Ticonderoga episode occupied perhaps a month. At the time Ethan was a man of thirty-seven. He had spent three quarters of his life unconsciously preparing himself for such an opportunity.

He came of Yoeman stock. Before emigrating to America with the Dorchester Company in 1632, the Allens owned land in Essexshire. They were Church of England separatists. After their exodus they, like the children of Israel, raised large families and moved. Four generations averaged ten children each and lived in eight different places. According to the town records of Litchfield, Connecticut, Ethan was born there January 10th, 1737 (old time).

Less than two years later he was carried in his mother's arms across the hills to Cornwall, the new town on the Housatonic. His childhood was spent in that log cabin frontier settlement. Dogs and pigs ran loose in the mud lane. Wolves howled in the forest nearby. There were Indian massacres in neighboring villages — even a witch, Moll Cramer, shunned and feared, living with her child in a solitary cabin not far away.

While a country is being settled there is always speculation in wild lands. Debts, crop failures, mistakes and misfortunes are continually forcing men and women from the old settlements out beyond the frontier to start life over again in the wilderness with a gun, an ax, a plow, a few seeds and a great deal of hope. Bright young men go ahead, pick out attractive sites, obtain grants from Governors or proprietors, and survey lots which they are prepared to sell to would-be pioneers.

After a brief service in the French and Indian War, some experience as manager of a Furnace in Salisbury and overseer of a lead mine in Northampton, Ethan became a land speculator. The Peace of Paris opened for settlement the region situated north of Massachusetts Bay between Lake Champlain and the Connecticut River. Its jurisdiction was in dispute. Although the Board of Trade had alloted it to New York Province, the governor of New Hampshire continued to grant townships within the district. In partnership with his brothers and a cousin, Remember Baker, he formed the Onion River Company and obtained from the New Hampshire Proprietors hundreds of Rights (a Right was usually 360 acres) of land in the vicinity of what is now Burlington, Vermont. When the New York grantees of the disputed region began to press their claims, Ethan organized among the settlers who had bought the land which

A
NARRATIVE
OF
Colonel ETHAN ALLEN's
CAPTIVITY,

From the Time of his being taken by the British, near Montreal, on the 25th Day of September, in the Year 1775, to the Time of his Exchange, on the 6th Day of May, 1778:

CONTAINING,

HIS VOYAGES AND TRAVELS,

With the most remarkable Occurrences respecting himself and many other Continental Prisoners of different Ranks and Characters, which fell under his Observation, in the Course of the same; particularly the Destruction of the Prisoners at New York, by General Sir William Howe, in the Years 1776 and 1777.

Interspersed with some POLITICAL OBSERVATIONS.

Written by himself, and now published for the Information of the Curious in all Nations.—*Price Ten Paper Dollars.*

When God from Chaos gave this World TO BE,
Man then he form'd, and form'd him TO BE FREE.
American Independence, a Poem, by FRENEAU.

PHILADELPHIA:
PRINTED AND SOLD BY ROBERT BELL, IN THIRD STREET.
M,DCC,LXXIX.

they had cleared and improved from the New Hampshire Proprietors, a band of minutemen who called themselves Green Mountain Boys and who for several years successfully withstood the Yorkers' attacks. Their leader was outlawed and posted. He escaped attempts to kidnap him, offered a reward for the capture of the Attorney General of New York Province and built a block fort to insure the validity of his land titles. When hostilities broke out between the King's troops and the farmers of Lexington, Ethan had at his command an organized army all ready to follow him to the King's forts situated at Ticonderoga and Crown Point — so dangerously close to the Onion River Company's land.

In the "Narrative" Ethan described the reduction of Ticonderoga and Lake Champlain, an attempt on Montreal, his capture, and captivity, covering the period from May, 1775 to May, 1778. The book was written about a year later and published as a serial in the "Pennsylvania Packet" beginning with the number of March, 1779. It was immediately afterwards issued as a book by Robert Bell at Philadelphia "Price Ten Paper Dollars". Because of its vivid and picturesque style, it became a best-seller: there were eight editions, in book form, within the first two years. Its popularity greatly helped Washington's efforts to save the languishing American cause from subsiding altogether.

Although the "Narrative" must have been written almost entirely from memory, a careful examination of contemporary documents has disclosed to this writer no substantial errors on the part of its author. The "Connecticut Courant" at Hartford, the "Massachusetts Spy" at Worcester, the "Pennsylvania Packet" at Philadelphia, etc., printed accounts of the capture of Ticonderoga with slight variations as to the number of men engaged, adding italicized comments such as "What think ye of the Yankees now?". Lieutenant Feltham, the second in command, sent a very careful report to General Gage which on the whole substantiates Ethan's account, though it implies that Arnold had a joint command and that Ethan at first mistook Feltham for his commander, Captain Delaplace. John Leacock's play "The Fall of British Tyranny" published in 1776 describes Ethan's interview with General Prescott at Montreal in almost the exact words used by Ethan in the "Narrative" three years later.

The fact, however, that none of these mentions Ethan's famous words "In the Name of the Great Jehovah and the Continental Congress" has lead recent historians to doubt their authenticity. It is the opinion of this writer that a man's statement of his own words should be accepted unless he is an habitual liar or there is conclusive evidence to the contrary. As shown above, the veracity of the rest of the "Narrative" is substantiated by contemporary documents. The evidence against Ethan's speech is entirely negative. On careful consideration it seems likely that Feltham reporting to the Commander-in-Chief would—as he did—mention that Ethan said he came from Connecticut, Arnold from Massachusetts, etc., and omit epigrams and oaths (there must have been many) shouted during the actual encounter. When the "Narrative" appeared in 1779, most of the participants were alive and able to read it, yet no doubt was cast upon its authenticity until many years later. On other similar occasions, Ethan used Biblical epithets—with similar success.

His later life (like his earlier years) was devoted to maintaining the independence of the New Hampshire Grants and the validity of the Onion River titles. He had to face the opposition of the British army in Canada as well as the New York delegation at Congress. The upshot of his efforts was the State of Vermont, admitted to the Union in 1791, two years after his death. His last days were spent on a farm, studying and writing philosophy. His extraordinary career included mining, manufacturing, real estate, fighting, imprisonment, statesmanship, diplomacy, farming and philosophy, but its most dramatic moments were certainly those described in the "Narrative".

J. P.

Fort Ticonderoga, N. Y.
October, 1929

Preface to the Walpole Edition : 1807

IN *announcing the publication of this little, simple, true and unvarnished Narrative, the publishers have complied with the wishes of a number of persons, who had a desire to keep in remembrance the hero of Ticonderoga, and the exploits he performed. It is believed that there is not a copy for sale in any bookstore in the United States; and the style of printing, at the time of its first appearance, which is now near thirty years since, was in so unimproved a condition, that it has never been seen but in the shabby dress of a large and ragged pamphlet. The events of those " troublous times," in which Col. Allen took a conspicuous part, are rendered doubly interesting from the lively, unadorned manner of his narration. The high compliments which he pays to the prowess, uniform perseverance and resolution, manifested by the " Green Mountain Boys " of his native State, will no doubt be an inducement to them, and to his countrymen generally, to read and preserve this monument of him, and as they con the pages of this "little book" which he has "left them," to imitate the coolness and courage of the deceased veteran. The sufferings and cruelties borne by him and his fellow soldiers; frequently draw from him in the course of his Narrative, a language the most severe, with respect to a country from whom we originated, with whom we are now at peace, and with whom it is our policy to continue on a friendly footing; but the candid and the feeling mind should make great allowance for the unparalleled situation of our affairs, for the sufferings of his handful of little "Spartans," for whom he felt a father's and a brother's affection. These circumstances must have given a deep colouring to the pencil which was pourtraying his own and his country's wrongs. On the whole, we think this little tract may be reperused, with advantage and pleasure, by the aged, and read with much edification and entertainment by the young. As it is deemed that the very words, in every respect, made use of by the Colonel, would be more acceptable to the reader, than any artificial decoration of style, we shall almost invariably adhere to the original.*

Walpole, N.H., 1807.

A NARRATIVE OF ETHAN ALLEN'S CAPTIVITY

INTRODUCTION

INDUCED by a sense of duty to my country, and by the application of many of my worthy friends, some of whom are of the first characters, I have concluded to publish the following narrative of the extraordinary scenes of my captivity, and the discoveries which I made in the course of the same, of the cruel and relentless disposition and behaviour of the enemy, towards the prisoners in their power; from which the state politician, and every gradation of character among the people, to the worthy tiller of the soil, may deduce such inferences as they shall think proper to carry into practice. Some men are appointed into office, in these States, who read the history of the cruelties of this war with the same careless indifferency, as they do the pages of the Roman history; nay, some are preferred to places of trust and profit by the tory influence. The instances are (I hope) but rare; and it stands all freemen in hand, to prevent their further influence, which, of all other things, would be the most baneful to the liberties and happiness of this country; and so far as such influence takes place, robs us of the victory we have obtained, at the expense of so much blood and treasure.

I should have exhibited to the public a history of the facts herein contained, soon after my exchange, had not the urgency of my private affairs, together with more urgent public business, demanded my attention, till a few weeks before the date hereof. The reader will readily discern, that a narrative of this sort could not have been wrote when I was a prisoner: My trunk and writings were often searched under various pretences; so that I never wrote a syllable, or made even a rough minute, whereon I might predicate this narration, but trusted solely to my memory for the whole. I have, however, taken the greatest care and pains to recollect the facts, and arrange them; but as they touch a variety of characters and opposite interests, I am sensible that all will not be pleased with the relation of them: Be this as it will, I have made truth my invariable guide, and stake my honor on the truth of the facts. I have been very generous with the British, in giving them full and ample credit for all their good usage of any considerable consequence, which I met with among them, during my captivity; which was easily done, as I met with but little, in comparison of the bad, which by reason of the great plurality of it, could not be contained in so concise a narrative; so that I am certain that I have more fully enumerated the favours which I received, than the abuses I suffered. The critic will be pleased to excuse any inaccuracies in the performance itself, as the author has unfortunately missed a liberal education.

ETHAN ALLEN

Bennington, March 25, 1779.

A Narrative

OF

COLONEL ETHAN ALLEN'S

OBSERVATIONS DURING

HIS CAPTIVITY

EVER since I arrived to a state of manhood, and acquainted myself with the general history of mankind, I have felt a sincere passion for liberty. The history of nations doomed to perpetual slavery, in consequence of yielding up to tyrants their natural born liberties, I read with a sort of philosophical horror; so that the first systematical and bloody attempt at Lexington, to enslave America, thoroughly electrified my mind, and fully determined me to take part with my country: And while I was wishing for an opportunity to signalize myself in its behalf, directions were privately sent to me from the then colony (now state) of Connecticut, to raise the Green Mountain Boys; (and if possible) with them to surprise and take the fortress Ticonderoga. This enterprise I cheerfully undertook; and, after first guarding all the several passes that led thither, to cut off all intelligence between the garrison and the country, made a forced march from Bennington, and arrived at the lake opposite to Ticonderoga, on the evening of the ninth day of May, 1775, with two hundred and thirty valiant Green Mountain Boys; and it was with the utmost difficulty that I procured boats to cross the lake: However, I landed eighty-three men near the garrison, and sent the boats back for the rear guard commanded by col. Seth Warner; but the day began to dawn, and I found myself under a necessity to attack the fort, before the rear could cross the lake; and, as it was viewed hazardous, I harangued the officers and soldiers in the manner following; "Friends and fellow soldiers, you have, for a "number of years past, been a scourge and ter- "ror to arbitrary power. Your valour has been "famed abroad, and acknowledged, as appears "by the advice and orders to me (from the gen-

[6]

The Honble
Jonathan Trumbull Esqr
Capt General & governor of the
Colony of Connecticut

Ticonderoga 12th. May 1775

Honob.l Sir I make You a Present of a Major
a Captain and Two Lieuts in the regular
Establishment of George the Third I hope
they may serve as ranforms for some of our
Friends at Boston and particularly for Cap
Brown of Rhodiseland a Party of men unde
the Command of Capt Herick has Took Posse
=sion Scanesborough Imprisoned Major sceer
and seized a Schooner of his, I Expect in
Ten days Time to have it rigged and mann
and Armed with 6 or 8 Pieces of Canon whic
with the Boats in our Possession I Purpose
to make an Attack on the armed Sloop of
George the Third which is Now Cruising
on Lake Champlain and is about Twice
as bigg as the Schooner, I Hope in a Short
Time to be Authorised to acquaint Your Hon=
=our that Lake Champlain & the fortifications
thereon are Subjected to the Colonies
The Enterprise has been Approbated by the

Officers and Soldiery of the Green Mountain
Boys Nor do I hisitate as to the Success
I Expect Lives must be Lost in the
attack as the Comander of Georges Sloop
is a man of Courage &c,

       I Conclude Capt Worner
is by this time in Possession of Crown Point
the Ordnance Stores &c I Conclude Governor
Carlton will Exert himself to oppose us &
Command the Lake &c — Messers Hickok
Kelsey — & Nichols have the Charge of Condu
cting the Officers to Hartford These Gentle
men have been Very Assiduous and active in
the Late Expadition I Depend upon Your
Honours aid and Assistance in a Situation
so Contiguous to ~~——————~~ Canada —
I Subscribe my self Your Honours Ever
Faithfull most Obedient and Humble Servant

             Ethan Allen

at Present Commander of Ticonderoga

"eral assembly of Connecticut) to surprise and
"take the garrison now before us. I now propose
"to advance before you, and in person conduct
"you through the wicket-gate; for we must this
"morning either quit our pretensions to valour,
"or possess ourselves of this fortress in a few min-
"utes; and, in as much as it is a desperate attempt,
"(which none but the bravest of men dare under-
"take) I do not urge it on any contrary to his
"will. You that will undertake voluntarily, poise
"your firelocks."

The men being (at this time) drawn up in
three ranks, each poised his firelock. I ordered
them to face to the right; and, at the head of the
centre-file, marched them immediately to the
wicket gate aforesaid, where I found a centry
posted, who instantly snapped his fusee at me; I
ran immediately toward him, and he retreated
through the covered way into the parade within
the garrison, gave a halloo, and ran under a
bomb-proof. My party who followed me into the
fort, I formed on the parade in such a manner as
to face the two barracks which faced each other.
The garrison being asleep, (except the centries)
we gave three huzzas which greatly surprised

them. One of the centries made a pass at one of my officers with a charged bayonet, and slightly wounded him: My first thought was to kill him with my sword; but, in an instant, altered the design and fury of the blow to a slight cut on the side of the head; upon which he dropped his gun, and asked quarter, which I readily granted him, and demanded of him the place where the commanding officer kept; he shewed me a pair of stairs in the front of a barrack, on the west part of the garrison, which led up to a second story in said barrack, to which I immediately repaired, and ordered the commander (capt. Delaplace) to come forth instantly, or I would sacrifice the whole garrison; at which the capt. came immediately to the door with his breeches in his hand, when I ordered him to deliver to me the fort instantly, who asked me by what authority I demanded it; I answered, "In the "name of the great Jehovah, and the Continental "Congress." (The authority of the Congress being very little known at that time) he began to speak again; but I interrupted him, and with my drawn sword over his head, again demanded an immediate surrender of the garrison; to which

[8]

I answered, "In the name of the great Jehovah, and the Continental Congress."

he then complied, and ordered his men to be forthwith paraded without arms, as he had given up the garrison; in the mean time some of my officers had given orders, and in consequence thereof, sundry of the barrack doors were beat down, and about one third of the garrison imprisoned, which consisted of the said commander, a lieut. Feltham, a conductor of artillery, a gunner, two serjeants, and forty four rank and file; about one hundred pieces of cannon, one 13 inch mortar, and a number of swivels. This surprise was carried into execution in the gray of the morning of the 10th day of May, 1775. The sun seemed to rise that morning with a superior lustre; and Ticonderoga and its dependencies smiled on its conquerors, who tossed about the flowing bowl, and wished success to Congress, and the liberty and freedom of America. Happy it was for me (at that time) that the then future pages of the book of fate, which afterwards unfolded a miserable scene of two years and eight months imprisonment, was hid from my view: But to return to my narration; col. Warner, with the rear guard crossed the lake, and joined me early in the morning, whom I sent off, without loss of time, with about one hundred men, to take possession of Crown Point, which was garrisoned with a serjeant and twelve men; which he took possession of the same day, as also upwards of one hundred pieces of cannon. But one thing now remained to be done, to make ourselves complete masters of lake Champlain: This was to possess ourselves of a sloop of war, which was then laying at St. John's; to effect which, it was agreed in a council of war, to arm and man out a certain schooner, which lay at South Bay, and that capt. (now general) Arnold should command her, and that I should command the batteaux. The necessary preparations being made, we set sail from Ticonderoga, in quest of the sloop, which was much larger, and carried more guns and heavier metal than the schooner. General Arnold, with the schooner sailing faster than the batteaux, arrived at St. John's; and by surprise possessed himself of the sloop, before I could arrive with the batteaux: He also made prisoners of a serjeant and twelve men, who were garrisoned at that place. It is worthy remark, that as soon as general Arnold had secured the prisoners on board, and had made preparation for sailing, the wind which but a few hours before was fresh in the south, and well served to carry us to St. John's, now shifted, and came fresh from the north; and in about one hours time, general Arnold sailed with the prize and schooner for Ticonderoga: When I met him with my party, within a few miles of St. John's, he saluted me with a discharge of cannon, which I returned with a volley of small arms: This being repeated three times, I went on board the sloop with my party, where several loyal Congress healths were drank. We were now masters of lake Champlain, and the garrisons depending thereon. This success I viewed of consequence in the scale of American politics; for if a settlement between the then colonies and Great Britain, had soon taken place, it would have been easy to have restored these acquisitions; but viewing the then future consequences of a cruel war, (as it has really proved to be) and the command of that lake, garrisons, artillery, &c. must be viewed to be of signal importance to the American cause, and it is marvellous to me, that we ever lost the command of it. Nothing but the taking a Burgoyne, with a whole British army, could (in my opinion) atone for it; and notwithstanding such an extraordinary victory, we must be obliged to regain the command of that lake again, be the cost what it will: By doing this, Canada will easily be brought into union and confederacy with the United States of America. Such an event would put it out of the power of the western tribes of Indians to carry on a war with us, and be a solid and durable bar against any further inhuman barbarities committed on our frontier inhabitants, by cruel and blood thirsty savages: for it is impossible for them to carry on a war, except they are supported by the trade and commerce of some civilized nation; which to them would be impracticable, did Canada compose a part of the American empire.

Early in the fall of the year, the little army, under the command of the generals Schuyler and Montgomery, were ordered to advance into Canada. I was at Ticonderoga, when this order arrived; and the general with most of the officers, requested me to attend them in the expedition; and though at that time, I had no commission from Congress, yet they engaged me, that I should be considered as an officer the same as though I had a commission; and should, as occasion might require, command certain detachments of the army. This I considered as an honourable offer, and did not hesitate to comply with it, and advanced with the army to the isle Auix Noix: from whence I was ordered (by the general) to go in company with major Brown, and certain interpreters, through the woods into Canada, with letters to the Canadians, and to let them know, that the design of the army was only against the English garrisons, and not the country, their liberties, or religion; And having, through much danger negociated this business, I returned to the isle Auix Noix in the fore part of September, when general Schuyler returned to Albany; and in consequence the command devolved upon general Montgomery, whom I assisted in laying a line of circumvallation round the fortress St. John's: After which I was ordered by the general, to make a second tour into Canada, upon nearly the same design as before; and withal to observe the disposition, designs and movement of the inhabitants of the country; This reconnoitre I undertook with reluctance, chusing rather to assist at the siege of St. John's, which was then closely invested; but my esteem for the general's person, and opinion of him as a politician and brave officer, induced me to proceed.

I passed through all the parishes on the river Sorrel, to a parish at the mouth of the same, which is called by the same name, preaching politics; and went from thence across the Sorrel to the river St. Lawrence, and up the river through the parishes to Longale, and so far met with good success as an itinerant. In this round, my guard was Canadians, (my interpreter and some few attendants excepted). On the morning of the 24th day of September, I set out with my guard of about eighty men, from Longale, to go to Lapraier; from whence I determined to go to general Montgomery's camp; but had not advanced two miles before I met with major Brown, (who has since been advanced to the rank of a Col.) who desired me to halt, saying that he had something of importance to communicate to me and my confidents; upon which I halted the party, and went into an house, and took a private room with him and several of my associates, where colonel Brown proposed, that "Provided I would return to Longale, and procure some canoes, so as to cross the river St. Lawrence a little north of Montreal, he would cross it a little to the south of the town, with near two hundred men, as he had boats sufficient; and that we would make ourselves masters of Montreal." . . . This plan was readily approved by me and those in council; and in consequence of which I returned to Longale collected a few canoes, and added about thirty English Americans to my party, and crossed the river in the night of the 24th, agreeable to the before proposed plan. My whole party, at this time, consisted of about one hundred and ten men, near eighty of whom were Canadians. We were the most of the night crossing the river, as we had so few canoes that they had to pass and re-pass three times, to carry my party across. Soon after day break, I set a guard between me and the town, with special orders, to let no person whatever pass or re-pass them, and another guard on in the other end of the road, with like directions; the mean time, I reconnoitered the best ground to make a defence expecting colonel Brown's party was landed on the other side of the town, he having (the day before) agreed to give three huzzas with his men early in the morning, which signal I was to return, that we might each know that both parties were landed; but the sun by this time being near two hours high, and the sign failing, I began to conclude myself to be in a premunire, and would have crossed the river back again, but I knew the enemy would have discovered such an attempt; and as there could not more than one third part of my troops cross at one time, the other two thirds would of course fall into their hands. This I could not reconcile to my own feelings as a man, much less as an officer: I therefore concluded to maintain the ground, (if possible) and all to fare alike. In consequence of this resolution, I dispatched two messengers, one to Lapraire, (to col. Brown) and the other to Lasumprion, (a French settlement) to Mr. Walker, who was in our interest, requesting their speedy assistance; giving them at the same time, to understand my critical situation: In the mean time, sundry persons came to my guards, pretending to be friends, but were by them taken prisoners and brought to me. These I ordered to confinement, 'till their friendship could be further confirmed; for I was jealous they were spies, as they proved to be afterwards: One of the principal of them making his escape, exposed the weakness of my party, which was the final cause of my misfortune; for I have been since informed that Mr. Walker, agreeable to my desire, exerted himself, and had raised a considerable number of men for my assistance, which brought him into difficulty afterwards; but upon hearing of my misfortune, disbanded them again.

The town of Montreal was in a great tumult. Gen. Carlton and the royal party made every preparation to go on board their vessels of force, (as I was afterwards informed) but the spy escaping from my guard to the town, occasioned an alteration in their policy, and emboldened Gen. Carlton to send the force, which he had there collected, out against me. I had previously chosen my ground, but when I saw the number of the enemy, as they sallied out of the town, I perceived it would be a day of trouble, if not of rebuke; but I had no chance to fly, as Montreal was situated on an island, and the river St. Lawrence cut off my communication to Gen. Montgomery's camp. I encouraged my soldiery to bravely defend themselves, that we should soon have help, and that we should be able to keep the ground, if no more. This, and much more I affirmed with the greatest seeming assurance, and which in reality I thought to be in some degree probable.

The enemy consisted of not more than forty regular troops, together with a mixed multitude, chiefly Canadians, with a number of English who lived in the town, and some Indians; in all to the number of 500.

The reader will notice that most of my party were Canadians; indeed it was a motley parcel of soldiery which composed both parties. However, the enemy began the attack from wood-piles, ditches, buildings, and such like places, at a considerable distance, and I returned the fire from a situation more than equally advantageous. The attack began between two and three of the clock in the afternoon, just before which I ordered a volunteer, by the name of Richard Young, with a detachment of nine men as a flank guard, which, under the cover of the bank of the river, could not only annoy the enemy, but at the same time, serve as a flank guard to the left of the main body.

The fire continued for some time on both sides; and I was confident that such a remote method of attack, could not carry the ground, (provided it should be continued till night): but near half the body of the enemy began to flank round to my right: upon which I ordered a volunteer, by the name of John Dugan, who had lived many years in Canada, and understood the French language, to detach about fifty of the Canadians, and post himself at an advantageous ditch, which was on my right to prevent my being surrounded: he advanced with the detachment, but instead of occupying the post, made his escape, as did likewise Mr. Young upon the left, with their detachments. I soon perceived that the enemy was in possession of the ground, which Dugan should have occupied. At this time I had but forty-five men with me; some of whom were wounded: the enemy kept closing round me, nor was it in my power to prevent it, by which means, my situation which was advantageous in the first part of the attack, ceased to be so in the last; and being almost entirely surrounded but with such vast unequal numbers, I ordered a retreat, but found that those of the enemy, who were of the country, and their Indians, could run as fast as my men, though the regulars could not. Thus I retreated near a mile, and some of the enemy, with the savages, kept flanking me, and others crowded hard in the rear: in fine I expected in a very short time, to try the world of spirits; for I was apprehensive that no quarter would be given to me, and therefore had determined to sell my life as dear as I could. One of the enemy's officers boldly pressing in the rear, discharged his fusee at me; the ball whistled near me, as did many others that day. I returned the salute, and missed him, as running had put us both out of breath; for I conclude we were not frightened, I then saluted him with my tongue in a harsh manner, and told him that inasmuch as his numbers were so far superior to mine, I would surrender, provided I could be treated with honor, and be assured of good quarter for myself and the men who were with me, and he answered I should; another officer coming up directly after, confirmed the treaty; upon which I agreed to surrender with my party, which then consisted of thirty-one effective men, and seven wounded. I ordered them to ground their arms, which they did.

The officer I capitulated with, then directed me and my party to advance towards him, which was done, I handed him my sword, and in half a minute after a savage, part of whose head was shaved, being almost naked and painted, with feathers intermixed with the hair of the other side of his head, came running to me with an incredible swiftness; he seemed to advance with more than mortal speed (as he approached near me, his hellish visage was beyond all description, snakes eyes appear innocent in comparison of his, his features extorted, malice, death, murder, and the wrath of devils and damned spirits are the emblems of his countenance) and in less than twelve feet of me, presented his firelock; at the instant, of his present, I twitched the officer to whom I gave my sword, between me and the savage, but he flew round with great fury, trying to single me out to shoot me without killing the officer; but by this time I was near as nimble as he, keeping the officer in such a position that his danger was my defence, but in less than half a minute, I was attacked by just such another imp of hell; then I made the officer fly around with incredible velocity, for a few seconds of time, when I perceived a Canadian (who had lost one eye, as appeared afterwards) taking my part against the savages; and in an instant an Irishman came to my assistance with a fixed bayonet, and drove away the fiends, swearing by Jasus he would kill them. This tragic scene composed my mind. The escaping from so awful a death, made even imprisonment happy, the more so as my conquerors on the field treated me with great civility and politeness.

The regular officers said that they were very happy to see Col. Allen, I answered them that I should rather chose to have seen them at Gen. Montgomery's camp; the gentlemen replied, that they gave full credit to what I said, and as I walked to the town, which was (as I should guess) more than two miles, a British officer walking at my right hand, and one of the French noblesse at my left; the latter of which in the action, had his eyebrow carried away by a glancing shot, but was nevertheless very merry and facetious, and

"*He flew round with great fury, trying to single me out to shoot me without killing the officer.*"

no abuse was offered me till I came to the barrack-yard at Montreal, where I met Gen. Prescott, who asked me my name, which I told him, he then asked me, whether I was that Col. Allen, who took Ticonderoga, I told him I was the very man; then he shook his cane over my head, calling many hard names, among which he frequently used the word rebel, and put himself in a great rage. I told him he would do well not to cane me, for I was not accustomed to it, and shook my fist at him, telling him that that was the beetle of mortality for him, if he offered to strike; upon which Capt. M'Cloud of the British, pulled him by the skirt, and whispered to him (as he afterwards told me) to this import; that it was inconsistent with his honor to strike a prisoner. He then ordered a sergeant's command with fixed bayonets to come forward and kill 13 Canadians, which were included in the treaty aforesaid.

It cut me to the heart to see the Canadians in so hard a case, in consequence of their having been true to me; they were wringing their hands, saying their prayers, (as I concluded) and expected immediate death. I therefore stepped be-

between the executioners and the Canadians, opened my clothes, and told Gen. Prescott to thrust his bayonets into my breast, for I was the sole cause of the Canadians taking up arms.

The guard in the mean time, rolling their eyeballs from the General to me, as though impatient waiting his dread commands to sheath their bayonets in my heart; I could however plainly discern, that he was in a suspence and quandary about the matter: this gave me additional hopes of succeeding, for my design was not to die but save the Canadians by a finesse. The General stood a minute, when he made the following reply: "I will not execute you now, but you shall grace a halter at Tyburn, God damn ye."

I remember I disdained his mentioning such a place, I was notwithstanding a little inwardly pleased with the expression, as it significantly conveyed to me the idea of postponing the present appearance of death; besides his sentence was by no means final, as to "gracing a halter," although I had anxiety about it after I landed in England, as the reader will find in the course of this history. Gen. Prescott then ordered one of his officers to take me on board the Gaspee schooner of War, and confine me, hands and feet, in irons, which was done the same afternoon I was taken.

The action continued an hour and three quarters by the watch, and I know not to this day how many of my men were killed, though I am certain there were but few; if I remember right, seven were wounded, one of them, William Stewart by name, was wounded by a savage with a tomahawk, after he was taken prisoner and disarmed, but was rescued by some of the generous enemy; and so far recovered his wounds, that he afterwards went with the other prisoners to England.

Of the enemy were killed a major Carden, who had been wounded in eleven different battles, and an eminent merchant, Patterson of Montreal, and some others, but I never knew their whole loss, as their accounts were different. I am apprehensive that it is rare, that so much ammunition was expended, and so little execution done by it; though such of my party as stood the ground, behaved with great fortitude, much exceeding that of the enemy, but were not the best of marksmen, and I am apprehensive, were

[25]

all killed or taken: the wounded were all put into the hospital at Montreal, and those that were not, were put on board of different vessels in the river and shackled together by pairs, viz. two men fastened together by one hand cuff, being closely fixed to one wrist of each of them, and treated with the greatest severity, nay as criminals.

I now come to the description of the irons, which were put on me; the hand cuff was of a common size and form, but my leg irons (I should imagine) would weigh thirty pounds; the bar was eight feet long, and very substantial; the shackles which encompassed my ancles, were very tight I was told by the officer who put them on, that it was the king's plate, and I heard other of their officers say, that it would weigh forty weight. The irons were so close upon my ancles, that I could not lie down in any other manner than on my back, I was put into the lowest and most wretched part of the vessel, where I got the favour of a chest to sit on, the same answered for my bed at night, and having procured some little blocks of the guard (who day and night, with fixed bayonets, watched over me) to lay under each end of the large bar of my leg irons, to preserve my ancles from galling, while I sat on the chest, or lay back on the same, though most of the time, night and day, I sat on it; but at length having a desire to lay down on my side, which the closeness of the irons forbid, desired the Captain to loosen them for that purpose, but was denied the favor: the Captain's name was Royal, who did not seem to be an ill natured man; but often times said, that his express orders were to treat me with such severity, which was disagreeable to his own feelings; nor did he ever insult me, though many others who came on board did. One of the officers, by the name of Bradley, was very generous to me, he would often send me victuals from his own table; nor did a day fail, but that he sent me a good drink of grog.

The reader is now invited back to the time I was put in irons. I requested the privilege to write to Gen. Prescott, which was granted. I reminded him of the kind and generous manner of my treatment to the prisoners I took at Ticonderoga; the injustice and ungentleman like usage, which I had met with from him, and demanded

[27]

gentleman like usage, but received no answer from him. I soon after wrote to Gen. Carlton, which met the same success. In the mean while many of those who were permitted to see me, were very insulting.

I was confined in the manner I have related, on board the Gaspee schooner, about six weeks; during which time I was obliged to throw out plenty of extravagant language, which answered certain purposes, (at that time) better than to grace a history.

To give an instance upon being insulted, in a fit of anger I twisted off a nail with my teeth, which I took to be a ten-penny nail; it went through the mortise of the bar of my hand cuff, and at the same time I swaggered over those who abused me; particularly a Doctor Dace, who told me that I was outlawed by New York, and deserved death for several years past; was at last fully ripened for the halter, and in a fair way to obtain it: when I challenged him, he excused himself in consequence, as he said, of my being a criminal; but I flung such a flood of language at him that it shocked him and the spectators, for my anger was very great. I heard

[28]

one say, damn him can he eat iron? After that a small padlock was fixed to the hand cuff, instead of the nail, and as they were mean-spirited in their treatment to me; so it appeared to me, that they were equally timorous and cowardly.

I was after sent with the prisoners taken with me to an armed vessel in the river, which lay off against Quebec, under the command of Capt. M'Cloud of the British, who treated me in a very generous and obliging manner, and according to my rank; in about twenty-four hours I bid him farewell with regret; but my good fortune still continued; the name of the captain of the vessel I was put on board, was Little John, who, with his officers, behaved in a polite, generous and friendly manner. I lived with them in the cabin, and fared on the best, my irons being taken off, contrary to the order he had received from the commanding officer; but Capt. Little John swore, that a brave man should not be used as a rascal on board his ship.

Thus I found myself in possession of happiness once more, and the evils I had lately suffered, gave me an uncommon relish for it.

Captain Little John used to go to Quebec almost every day, in order to pay his respects to certain gentlemen and ladies; being there on a certain day, he happened to meet with some disagreeable treatment, as he imagined, from a lieutenant of a man of war, and one word brought on another till the lieutenant challenged him to a duel on the plains of Abraham. Captain Little John was a gentleman, who entertained a high sense of honour, and could do no less than accept the challenge.

At nine o'clock the next morning they were to fight. The Captain returned in the evening, and acquainted his lieutenant and me with the affair: his lieutenant was a high-blooded Scotchman as well as himself, who replied to his captain that he should not want for a second. With this I interrupted him, and gave the captain to understand, that since an opportunity had presented, I would be glad to testify my gratitude to him, by acting the part of a faithful second, on which he gave me his hand, and said that he wanted no better man. Says he, "I am a king's officer, and you a prisoner under my care; you must therefore go with me to the place appointed, in disguise;" and added further, "You must engage to me, upon the honour of a gentleman, that whether I die or live, or whatever happens, provided you live, that you will return to my lieutenant, on board this ship." All this I solemnly engaged him; the combatants were to discharge each a pocket pistol, and then to fall on with their iron-hilted muckle whangers; and one of that sort was allotted for me; but some British officers, who interposed early in the morning, settled the controversy without fighting.

Now having enjoyed eight or nine days happiness, from the polite and generous treatment of Captain Little John and his officers, I was obliged to bid them farewell, parting with them in as friendly a manner as we had lived together, which, to the best of my memory, was the eleventh of November, when a detachment of Gen. Arnold's little army appeared on Point Levy, opposite Quebec, who had performed an extraordinary march through a wilderness country, with design to have surprised the capital of Canada. I was then taken on board a vessel called the Adamant, together with the prisoners taken with me, and put under the power of an English merchant from London, whose name was Brook

Watson, a man of malicious and cruel disposition, and who was probably excited in the exercise of his malevolence, by a junto of tories, who sailed with him to England; among whom were Col. Guy Johnson, Col. Closs, and their attendants and associates, to the number of about thirty.

All the ship's crew (Col. Closs, in his personal behaviour, excepted) behaved towards the prisoners with that spirit of bitterness, which is the peculiar characteristic of tories, when they have the friends of America in their power, measuring their loyalty to the English king, by the barbarity, fraud, and deceit which they exercise towards the whigs.

A small place in the vessel, enclosed with white-oak plank, was assigned for the prisoners, and for me among the rest; I should imagine that it was no more than twenty feet one way, and twenty-two the other. Into this place we were all, to the number of thirty-four, thrust and hand-cuffed, (two prisoners more being added to our number) and were provided with two excrement tubs; in this circumference we were obliged to eat and perform the office of evacuation, during the voyage to England; and were insulted by every blackguard sailor and tory on board, in the cruelest manner; but what is the most surprising is, that not one of us died in the passage. When I was first ordered to go into the filthy inclosure, through a small sort of door, I positively refused, and endeavoured to reason the before named Brook Watson out of a conduct so derogatory to every sentiment of honour and humanity; but all to no purpose, my men being forced in the den already, and the rascal who had the charge of the prisoners commanded me to go immediately in among the rest; he further added, that the place was good enough for a rebel, that it was impertinent for a capital offender to talk of honour or humanity; that any thing short of a halter was too good for me, and that that would be my portion soon after I landed in England, for which purpose only I was sent thither. About the same time a lieutenant among the tories, insulted me in a grievous manner, saying that I ought to have been executed for my rebellion against New York, and spit in my face; upon which, though I was hand-cuffed, I sprang at him with both

[33]

hands, and knocked him partly down, but he scrambled along into the cabin, and I after him; there he got under the protection of some men with fixed bayonets, who were ordered to make ready to drive me into the place afore-mentioned. I challenged him to fight, notwithstanding the impediments that were on my hands, and had the exalted pleasure to see the rascal tremble for fear; his name I have forgot, but Watson ordered his guard to get me into the place with the other prisoners, dead or alive; and I had almost as leave die as do it, standing it out till they environed me round with bayonets; and brutish, prejudiced, abandoned wretches they were, from whom I could expect nothing but death or wounds: however, I told them, that they were good honest fellows, that I could not blame them, that I was only in a dispute with a callico merchant, who knew not how to behave towards a gentleman of the military establishment. This was spoke rather to appease them for my own preservation, as well as to treat Watson with contempt; but still I found that they were determined to force me into the wretched circumstances, which their prejudiced and depraved

"*I sprang at him with both hands and knocked him partly down.*"

minds had prepared for me: therefore rather than die, I submitted to their indignities, being drove with bayonets into the filthy dungeon, with the other prisoners, where we were denied fresh water, except a small allowance, which was very inadequate to our wants; and in consequence of the stench of the place, each of us was soon followed with a diarrhœa and fever, which occasioned an intolerable thirst. When we asked for water, we were most commonly (instead of obtaining it,) insulted and derided; and to add to all the horrors of the place, it was so dark that we could not see each other, and were overspread with body lice. We had, notwithstanding these severities, full allowance of salt provisions, and a gill of rum per day; the latter of which was of the utmost service to us, and probably was the means of saving several of our lives. About forty days we existed in this manner, when the land's end of England was discovered from the mast head; soon after which the prisoners were taken from their gloomy abode, being permitted to see the light of the sun, and breathe fresh air, which to us was very refreshing. The day following we landed at Falmouth.

[35]

A few days before I was taken prisoner, I shifted my cloaths, by which I happened to be taken in a Canadian dress, viz. a short fawn skin jacket, double-breasted, an under vest and breeches of sagathy, worsted stockings, a decent pair of shoes, two plain shirts, and a red worsted cap; this was all the cloathing I had, in which I made my appearance in England.

When the prisoners were landed, multitudes of the citizens of Falmouth, excited by curiosity, crowded together to see us, which was equally gratifying to us. I saw numbers of people on the tops of houses, and the rising adjacent grounds were covered with them of both sexes; the throng was so great, that the king's officers were obliged to draw their swords, and force a passage to Pendennis castle, which was near a mile from the town, where we were closely confined, in consequence of orders from Gen. Carlton, who then commanded in Canada.

The rascally Brook Watson then set out for London in great haste, expecting the reward of his zeal; but the ministry received him (as I have been since informed) rather coolly; for the minority in parliament took advantage, arguing

[36]

that the opposition of America to Great Britain, was not a rebellion. . . . "If it is," say they, "why do you not execute Col. Allen, according to law?". . . But the majority argued, that I ought to be executed, and that the opposition was really a rebellion, but that policy obliged them not to do it, inasmuch as the Congress had then most prisoners in their power; so that my being sent to England for the purpose of being executed, and necessity restraining them, was rather a foil on their laws and authority, and they consequently disapproved of my being sent thither. . . . But I never had heard the least hint of those debates in parliament, or of the working of their policy, till some time after I left England.

Consequently the reader will readily conceive I was anxious about my preservation, knowing that I was in the power of a haughty and cruel nation, and considered as such; therefore the first proposition which I determined in my own mind was, that humanity and moral suasion would not be consulted in the determination of my fate; and those that daily came in great numbers, out of curiosity to see me, both gentle and simple united in this, that I would be hanged.

A gentleman from America, by the name of Temple, and who was friendly to me, just whispered me in the ear, and told me, that bets were laid in London that I would be executed; he likewise privately gave me a guinea, but durst say but little to me.

However, agreeable to my first negative proposition, that moral virtue would not influence my destiny, I had recourse to stratagem, which I was in hopes would move in the circle of their policy. I requested of the commander of the castle the privilege of writing to Congress, who, after consulting with an officer that lived in town, of a superior rank, permitted me to write. I wrote, in the fore part of the letter, a short narrative of my ill treatment; but withal let them know, that though I was treated as a criminal in England, and continued in irons, together with those taken with me, yet it was in consequence of the orders which the commander of the castle received from Gen. Carlton; and therefore desired Congress to desist from matters of retaliation, till they should know the result of the government at England, respecting their treatment towards me, and the prisoners with me, and govern themselves accordingly; with a particular request, that if retaliation should be found necessary, that it might be exercised not according to the smallness of my character in America, but in proportion to the importance of the cause for which I suffered . . . this is, according to my present recollection, the substance of the letter, subscribed, "To the illustrious Continental Congress." This letter was wrote with a view that it should be sent to the ministry at London, rather than to Congress, with a design to intimidate the haughty English government, and screen my neck from the halter.

The next day the officer from whom I obtained licence to write, came to see me, and frowned on me on account of the impudence of the letter, (as he phrased it) and further added, "Do you think that we are fools in England, and would send your letter to Congress, with instructions to retaliate on our own people; I have sent your letter to Lord North." This gave me inward satisfaction, though I carefully concealed it with a pretended resentment, for I found I had come yankee over him, and that the letter had gone to the identical person I designed it for. Nor do I know, to this day, but that it had the desired effect, though I have not heard any thing of the letter since.

My personal treatment by lieutenant Hamilton, who commanded the castle, was very generous. He sent me every day a fine breakfast and dinner from his own table, and a bottle of good wine. Another aged gentleman, whose name I cannot recollect, sent me a good supper: but there was no distinction in public support between me and the privates; we all lodged on a sort of Dutch bunks, in one common apartment, and were allowed straw. The privates were well supplied with fresh provision, and, with me, took effectual measures to rid ourselves of lice.

I could not but feel inwardly extreme anxious for my fate; this I however carefully concealed from the prisoners, as well as from the enemy, who were perpetually shaking the halter at me. I nevertheless treated them with scorn and contempt; and having sent my letter to the ministry, could conceive of nothing more in my power but to keep up my spirits and behave in a daring soldier-like manner, that I might exhibit a good sample of American fortitude. Such a conduct I judged would have a more probable tendency to my preservation than concession and timidity. This, therefore, was my deportment, and I had lastly determined in my own mind, that if a cruel death must inevitably be my portion, I would face it undaunted, and though I greatly rejoice that I have returned to my country and friends, and to see the power and pride of Great Britain humbled, yet I am confident I could then die without the least appearance of dismay.

I now clearly recollect that my mind was so resolved, that I would not have trembled or shewn the least fear, as I was sensible it could not alter my fate, nor do more than reproach my memory, make my last act despicable to my enemies, and eclipse the other actions of my life. For I reasoned thus, that nothing was more common than for men to die, with their friends round them, weeping and lamenting over them, but not able to help them, which was in reality not different in the consequence of it from such a death as I was apprehensive of; and as death was the natural consequence of animal life to which the laws of nature subject mankind, to be timorous and uneasy as to the event or manner of it, was inconsistent with the character of a philosopher or soldier. The cause I was engaged in, I ever viewed worthy hazarding my life for, nor was I (at the critical moments of trouble) sorry that I engaged in it; and as to the world of spirits, though I knew nothing of the mode or manner of it, expected nevertheless, when I should arrive at such a world, that I should be as well treated as other gentlemen of my merit.

Among the great numbers of people, who came to the castle to see the prisoners, some gentlemen told me, that they had come 50 miles on purpose to see me, and desired to ask me a number of questions, and to make free with me in conversation. I gave for answer, that I chose freedom in every sense of the word: Then one of them asked me what my occupation in life had been? I answered him, that in my younger days I had studied divinity, but was a conjurer by passion. He replied, that I conjured wrong at the time that I was taken; and I was obliged to own, that I mistook a figure at that time, but that I had conjured them out of Ticonderoga. This was a place of great notoriety in England, so that the joke seemed to go in my favour.

It was a common thing for me to be taken out of close confinement, into a spacious green in the castle, or rather parade, where numbers of gentlemen and ladies were ready to see and hear me. I often entertained such audiences, with harangues on the impracticability of Great Britain's conquering the (then) colonies of America. At one of these times I asked a gentleman for a bowl of punch, and he ordered his servant to bring it, which he did, and offered it me, but I refused to take it from the hand of his servant; he then gave it to me with his own hand, refusing to drink with me in consequence of my being a state criminal: However I took the punch and drank it all down at one draught, and handed the gentleman the bowl: This made the spectators as well as myself merry.

I expatiated on American freedom: This gained the resentment of a young beardless gentleman of the company, who gave himself very great airs, and replied, that he "knew the Ameri-"cans very well, and was certain that they could "not bear the smell of powder." I replied, that I accepted it as a challenge, and was ready to convince him on the spot, that an American could

[43]

bear the smell of powder; at which he answered he should not put himself on a par with me. I then demanded of him to treat the character of the Americans with due respect: He answered that I was an Irishman; but I assured him, that I was a *full blooded Yankee*, and in fine, bantered him so much, that he left me in possession of the ground, and the laugh went against him. Two clergymen came to see me, and inasmuch as they behaved with civility, I returned them the same: We discoursed on several parts of moral philosophy and christianity; and they seemed to be surprized, that I should be acquainted with such topics, or that I should understand a syllogism or regular mood of argumentation. I am apprehensive my Canadian dress contributed not a little to the surprize, and excitement of curiosity: To see a gentleman in England, regularly dressed and well behaved, would be no sight at all; but such a rebel, as they were pleased to call me, it is probable was never before seen in England.

The prisoners were landed at Falmouth a few days before Christmas, and ordered on board of the Solebay frigate, Captain Symonds, the eighth day of January, 1776, when our hand irons were taken off. This remove was in consequence (as I have been since informed) of a writ of habeas corpus, which had been procured by some gentlemen in England, in order to obtain me my liberty.

The Solebay with several other men of war, and about forty transports, rendezvoused at the cove of Cork, in Ireland, to take in provision and water.

When we were first brought on board, Captain Symonds ordered all the prisoners, and most of the hands on board, to go on the deck, and caused to be read in their hearing, a certain code of laws, or rules for the regulation and ordering of their behaviour; and then in a sovereign manner, ordered the prisoners, me in particular, off the deck, and never to come on it again; for said he, this is a place for gentlemen to walk. So I went off, an officer following me, who told me, that he would shew me the place allotted for me, and took me down to the cable tire, saying to me, this is your place.

Prior to this I had taken cold, by which I was in an ill state of health, and did not say much to the officer; but stayed there that night, con-

[45]

sulted my policy, and found I was in an evil case; that a Captain of a man of war was more arbitrary than a king, as he could view his territory with a look of his eye, and a movement of his finger commanded obedience. . . . I felt myself more desponding than I had done at any time before; for I concluded it to be a governmental scheme, to do that clandestinely, which policy forbid me to be done under sanction of public justice and law.

However, two days after I shaved and cleansed myself as well as I could, and went on deck. The Captain spoke to me in a great rage, and said, "Did I not order you not to come on deck?" I answered him, that at the same time he said, "That it was a place for gentlemen to walk;" That I was Col. Allen, but had not been properly introduced to him. He replied, "G—d damn you, Sir, be careful not to walk the same side of the deck that I do." This gave encouragement, and ever after that I walked in the manner he had directed, except when he (at certain times afterwards) ordered me off in a passion, and then would directly afterwards go on again, telling him to command his slaves, that I was a gentleman, and had a right to walk the deck; yet when he expressly ordered me off, I obeyed, not out of obedience to him, but to set an example to his ship's crew, who ought to obey him.—

To walk to the windward side of the deck, is according to custom the prerogative of the Captain of the man of war, though he oftentimes, nay commonly walks with his Lieutenants, when no strangers are by; When a captain from some other man of war, comes on board, the Captains walk to the windward side, and the other gentlemen to the leeward.

It was but a few nights I lodged in the cable tire, before I gained acquaintance with the master of arms; his name was Gillegin, an Irishman, who was a generous and well disposed man, and in a friendly manner, made me a proffer of lying with him in a little birth, which was allotted him between decks, and enclosed with canvas; his preferment on board was about equal to that of a sergeant in a regiment, I was comparatively happy in the acceptance of his clemency, and lived with him in friendship, till the frigate anchored in the harbour of cape Fear, North Carolina, in America.

Nothing of material consequence happened 'till the fleet rendezvoused at the cove of Cork, (except a violent storm which brought old hardy sailors to their prayers). It was soon rumoured in Cork that I was on board the Solebay, with a number of prisoners from America; upon which Messrs. Clark and Hay, merchants in company, and a number of other benevolently disposed gentlemen, contributed largely to the relief and support of the prisoners, who were thirty-four in number, and in very needy circumstances. A suit of cloaths from head to foot, including an over coat, or surtout, with two shirts, were bestowed on each of them. My suit I received in super-fine broadcloath, sufficient for two jackets, and two pair of breeches overplus of a suit throughout, eight fine Holland shirts and stocks ready made, with a number of pairs of silk and worsted hose, two pair of shoes, two beaver hats, one of which was sent me richly laced with gold, by Mr. James Bonwell. The Irish gentlemen furthermore made a large gratuity of wines of the best sort, old spirits, Geneva, loaf and brown sugar, coffee, tea and chocolate, with a large round of pickled beef, and a number of fat turkies, with many other articles (for my sea stores) too tedious to mention here. To the privates they bestowed to each man two pounds of tea, and six pounds of brown sugar. These articles were received on board, (at a time when the Captain and first Lieut. were gone on shore) by permission of the second Lieut. a handsome young gentleman who was then under 20 years of age; his name was Douglass, the son of Admiral Douglass, (as I was informed).

As this munificence was so unexpected and plentiful, I may add needful, it impressed on my mind the highest sense of gratitude towards my benefactors; for I was not only supplied with the necessaries and conveniences of life, but with grandeurs and superfluities of it. Mr. Hays, one of the donators before mentioned, came on board, and behaved in the most obliging manner, telling me, that he hoped my troubles were past, for that the gentlemen of Cork determined to make my sea stores equal to the Captain of the Solebay's; he made a proffer of live stock, and wherewith to support them; but I knew this would be denied; And to crown all, did send to me by another person fifty guineas, but I could not reconcile the receiving the whole to my own feelings, as it might have the appearance of avarice, and therefore received but seven guineas only, and am confident not only from the exercise of the present well timed generosity, but from a large acquaintance with gentlemen of this nation, that as a people, they excel in liberality and bravery.

Two days after the receipt, of the aforesaid donations, Captain Symonds came on board, full of envy towards the prisoners, and swore by all that is good, that the damned American rebels should not be feasted at this rate, by the damned rebels of Ireland, he therefore took away all my liquors before mentioned, (except some of the wine which was secreted, and a two gallon jug of old spirits which was reserved for me, per favour of Lieut. Douglass.) The taking my liquors was abominable in his sight, he therefore spoke in my behalf, till the Captain was angry with him, and in consequence, proceeded and took away all the tea and sugar, which had been given to the other prisoners, and confiscated it to the use of the ship's crew. Our cloathing was not taken away, but the privates were forced to do duty on board. Soon after this there came a boat to the side of the ship, and Capt. Symonds asked a gentleman that was in it, (in my hearing) what his business was? who answered that he was sent to deliver some sea-stores to Col. Allen, which (if I remember right) he said were sent from Dublin, but the Captain damned him very heartily, ordered him away from the ship, and would not suffer him to deliver the stores. I was furthermore informed, that the gentlemen in Cork requested of Capt. Symonds that I might be allowed to come into the city, and that they would be responsible that I should return to the frigate at a given time, which was denied them.

We sailed from England the 8th day of January, and from the cove of Cork the 12th day of February. Just before we sailed, the prisoners with me were divided, and put on board three different ships of war. This gave me some uneasiness, for they were to a man zealous in the cause of liberty, and behaved with a becoming fortitude in the various scenes of their captivity, but those who were distributed on board other ships of war, were much better used than those that tarried with me, as appeared afterwards.

—— When the fleet consisting of about 45 sail, including 5 men of war, sailed from the cove with a fresh breeze, the appearance was beautiful, (abstracted from the unjust and bloody designs they had in view). We had not sailed many days, before a mighty storm arose, which lasted near 24 hours without intermission. The wind blew with relentless fury, and no man could remain on deck, except he was lashed fast, for the waves rolled over the deck by turns, with a forcible rapidity, and every soul on board was anxious for the preservation of the ship, (alias) their lives. In this storm the Thunder-bomb man of war sprang a leak, and was afterwards floated to some part of the coast of England, and the crew saved. We were then said to be in the bay of Biscay... After the storm abated, I could plainly discern that the prisoners were better used for some considerable time.

Nothing of consequence happened after this, till we had sailed to the island of Madeira, except a certain favour which I received of Captain Symonds, in consequence of an application I made to him, for the privilege of his tailor to make me a suit of cloaths of the cloth bestowed on me in Ireland, which he generously granted. I could then walk the deck with a seeming better grace. When we had reached Madeira, and anchored, sundry gentlemen with the Captain went on shore, who I conclude gave the rumour that I was in the frigate, upon which I soon after found that Irish generosity was again excited; for a gentleman of this nation sent his clerk on board, to know of me if I would accept a sea store from him (particularly of wine). This matter I made known to the generous Lieut. Douglass, who readily granted me the favour, provided the articles could be brought on board, during the time of his command, adding that it would be a pleasure to him to serve me, notwithstanding the opposition he met with before; So I directed the gentleman's clerk to inform him, that I was greatly in need of so signal a charity, and desired the young gentleman to make the utmost dispatch, which he did, but in the mean time, Capt. Symonds and his officers came on board, and immediately made ready for sailing; the wind at the same time being fair, set sail when the young gentleman was in fair sight with the aforesaid store.

The reader will doubtless recollect the seven guineas I received at the cove of Cork: These enabled me to purchase of the purser what I wanted, had not the capt. strictly forbid it, though I made sundry applications to him for that purpose; but his answer to me, when I was sick, was, that it was no matter how soon I was dead, and that he was no way anxious to preserve the lives of rebels, but wished them all dead; and indeed that was the language of most of the ship's crew. I expostulated not only with the capt. but with other gentlemen on board, on the unreasonableness of such usage; inferring, that inasmuch as the government in England did not proceed against me as a capital offender, they should not; for that they were by no means impowered by any authority, either civil or military, to do so; for the English government had acquitted me by sending me back a prisoner of war to America, and that they should treat me as such, I further drawed an inference of impolicy on them, provided they should, by hard usage, destroy my life; inasmuch as I might, if living, redeem one of their officers; but the capt. replied, that he needed no directions of mine

how to treat a rebel; that the British would conquer the American rebels, hang the Congress,
and such as promoted the rebellion, (me in particular) and retake their own prisoners; so that
my life was of no consequence in the scale of
their policy. I gave him for answer, that if they
stayed till they conquered America, before they
hanged me, *I should die of old age*, and desired
that till such an event took place, he would at
least allow me to purchase of the purser, for my
own money, such articles as I greatly needed;
but he would not permit it, and when I reminded him of the generous and civil usage that
their prisoners in captivity in America met with,
he said that it was not owing to their goodness,
but to their timidity; for, said he, they expect to
be conquered, and therefore dare not misuse
our prisoners, and in fact this was the language
of the British officers 'till gen. Burgoyne was
taken, (happy event) and not only of the officers,
but of the whole British Army. I appeal to all
my brother prisoners that have been with the
British in the southern department, for a con-
firmation of what I have advanced on this subject. The surgeon of the Solebay, whose name is

North, was a very humane and obliging man, and took the best care of the prisoners who were sick.

The third day of May we cast anchor in the harbour of cape Fear in North Carolina, as did Sir Peter Parker's ship of fifty guns, a little back of the bar, for there was no depth of water for him to come into the harbour: These two men of war and fourteen sale of transports and others came after, so that most of the fleet rendezvoused at cape Fear, for three weeks. The soldiers on board the transports were sickly, in consequence of so long a passage; add to this the small pox carried off many of them: They landed on the main, and formed a camp; but the riflemen annoyed them, and caused them to move to an island in the harbour; but such cursing of riflemen I never heard.

A detachment of regulars was sent up Brunswick river; as they landed, were fired on by those marksmen, and they came back next day damning the rebels for their unmanly way of fighting, and swearing that they would give no quarter, for they took sight at them, and were behind timber, skulking about. One of the de-

'tachments said they lost one man; but a negro man who was with them, and heard what was said, soon after told me that he helped to bury 31 of them; this did me some good to find my countrymen giving them battle; for I never heard such swaggering as among general Clinton's little army, (who commanded at that time) and I am apt to think there were 4000 men though not two thirds of them fit for duty. I heard numbers of them say, that the trees in America should hang well with fruit that campaign, for they would give no quarter; This was in the mouths of most whom I heard speak on the subject, officer as well as soldier. I wished at that time my countrymen new as well as I did what a murdering and cruel enemy they had to deal with; but experience has since taught this country, what they are to expect at the hands of Britons when in their power.

The prisoners who had been sent on board different men of war at the cove of Cork, were collected together, and the whole of them put on board the Mercury frigate, capt. James Montague, except one of the Canadians, who died on the passage from Ireland, and Peter

Noble, who made his escape from the Sphynx man of war in this harbour, and by extraordinary swimming got safe home to New England, and gave intelligence of the usage of his brother prisoners. The Mercury set sail from this port for Halifax, about the 20th of May, and Sir Peter Parker was about to sail with the land forces, under the command of gen. Clinton, for the reduction of Charlestown, the capital of South Carolina, and when I heard of his defeat in Halifax, it gave me inexpressible satisfaction.

I now found myself under a worse capt. than Symonds; for Montague was loaded with prejudices against every body; and every thing that was not stamped with royalty; and being by nature underwitted, his wrath was heavier than the others, or at least his mind was in no instance liable to be diverted by good sense, humour or bravery, of which Symonds was by turns susceptible. A capt. Francis Proctor was added to our number of prisoners when we were first put on board this ship: This gentleman had formerly belonged to the English service. The capt. and in fine all the gentlemen of the ship, were very much incensed against him, and put him in irons without the least provocation, and he was continued in this miserable situation about three months. In this passage the prisoners were infected with the scurvy, some more and some less, but most of them severely. The ships crew was to a great degree troubled with it, and I concluded that it was catching: Several of the crew died of it on their passage. I was weak and feeble in consequence of so long and cruel a captivity, yet had but little of the scurvy.

The purser was again expressly forbid by the capt. to let me have any thing out of his store; upon which I went on deck, and in the handsomest manner requested the favour of purchasing a few necessaries of the purser, which was denied me; he further told me, that I should be hanged as soon as I arrived at Halifax. I tried to reason the matter with him, but found him proof against reason; I also held up his honor to view, and his behaviour to me and the prisoners in general, as being derogatory to it, but found his honor impenetrable, I then endeavoured to touch his humanity, but found he had none; for his prepossession of bigotry to his own party, had confirmed him in an opinion, that no humanity was due to unroyalists, but seemed to think that heaven and earth were made merely to gratify the king and his creatures; he uttered considerable unintelligible and grovelling ideas, a little tinctured with monarchy, but stood well to his text of hanging me. He afterwards forbid his surgeon to administer any help to the sick prisoners. I was every night shut down in the cable tire, with the rest of the prisoners, and we lived miserable while under his power: But I received some generosity from several of the midshipmen, who in some degree alleviated my misery: one of their names was Putrass, the others I do not recollect; but they were obliged to be private in the bestowment of their favour, which was sometimes good wine bitters, and at others a generous drink of grog.

Sometime in the first week of June, we came to anchor at the Hook of New York, where we remained but three days; in which time governor Tryon, Mr. Kemp, the old attorney general of New York, and several other perfidious and over-grown tories and land-jobbers, came on board. Tryon viewed me with a stern countenance, as I was walking on the leeward side of the deck, with the midshipmen; and he and his companions were walking with the captain and lieutenant on the windward side of the same, but never spoke to me, though it is altogether probable that he thought of the old quarrel between him, the old government of New York, and the Green Mountain Boys: then they went with the captain into the cabin, and the same afternoon returned on board a vessel which lay near the Hook, where at that time they took sanctuary from the resentment of their injured country. What passed between the officers of the ship and these visitors I know not; but this I know, that my treatment from the principal officers was more severe afterwards.

We arrived at Halifax not far from the middle of June, where the ship's crew, which was infested with the scurvy, were taken on shore, and shallow trenches dug, into which they were put, and partly covered with earth; indeed, every proper measure was taken for their relief. The prisoners were not permitted any sort of medicine, but were put on board a sloop which lay in the harbour, near the town of Halifax, surrounded with several men of war and their tenders, and a guard constantly set over them, night and day. The sloop we had wholly to ourselves, except the guard who occupied the forecastle; here we were cruelly pinched with hunger; it seemed to me that we had not more than one third of the common allowance; we were all seized with violent hunger and faintness; we divided our scanty allowance as exact as possible. I shared the same fate with the rest, and though they offered me more than an even share, I refused to accept it, as it was a time of substantial distress, which in my opinion I ought to partake equally with the rest, and set an example of virtue and fortitude to our little commonwealth.

I sent letter after letter to Captain Montague, who still had the care of us, and also to his lieutenant, whose name I cannot call to mind, but could obtain no answer, much less a redress of grievances; and to add to the calamity, near a dozen of the prisoners were dangerously ill of the scurvy. I wrote private letters to the doctors, to procure, if possible, some remedy for the sick, but in vain. The chief physician came by in a boat so close that the oars touched the sloop we were in, and I uttered my complaint in the genteelest manner to him, but he never so much as turned his head, or made me any answer, though I continued speaking till he got out of hearing. Our cause then become very deplorable; still I kept writing to the captain, till he ordered the guards, as they told me, not to bring any more letters from me to him. In the mean time an event happened worth relating; one of the men almost dead of the scurvy, lay by the side of the sloop, and a canoe of Indians coming by, he purchased two quarts of strawberries, and eat them at once, and it almost cured him. The money he gave for them, was all the money he had in the world. After that he tried every way to procure more of that fruit, reasoning from analogy that they might have the same effect on others infested with the same disease, but could obtain none.

Meanwhile the doctor's mate of the Mercury came privately on board the prison sloop, and presented me with a large vial of smart drops, which proved to be good for the scurvy, though vegetables and some other ingredients were requisite for a cure; but the drops gave at least a

[63]

check to the disease. This was a well-timed exertion of humanity, (but the doctor's name has slipped my mind) and in my opinion was the means of saving the lives of several men.

The guard which was set over us, was by this time touched with the feelings of compassion; and I finally trusted one of them with a letter of complaint to Governor Arbuthnot of Halifax, which he found means to communicate, and which had the desired effect; for the governor sent an officer and surgeon on board the prison-sloop, to know the truth of the complaint. The officer's name was Russel, who held the rank of lieutenant, and treated me in a friendly and polite manner, and was really angry at the cruel and unmanly usage the prisoners met with; and with the surgeon made a true report of matters to Governor Arbuthnot, who either by his order or influence, took us next day from the prison-sloop to Halifax gaol, where I first became acquainted with the now Honourable James Lovel, Esq. one of the members of Congress for the state of Massachusetts Bay. The sick were taken to the hospital, and the Canadians who were effective, were employed in the king's works; and when their countrymen were recovered from the scurvy, and joined them, they all deserted the king's employ, and were not heard of at Halifax, as long as the remainder of the prisoners continued there, which was till near the middle of October. We were on board the prison-sloop about six weeks, and were landed at Halifax near the middle of August. Several of our English American prisoners, who were cured of the scurvy at the hospital, made their escape from thence, and after a long time reached their old habitations.

I had now but thirteen with me of those that were taken in Canada, and remained in gaol with me in Halifax, who in addition to those that were imprisoned before, made our number about thirty-four, who were all locked up in one common large room, without regard to rank, education, or any other accomplishment, where we continued from the setting to the rising sun; and as sundry of them were infected with the gaol and other distempers: the furniture of this spacious room consisted most principally of excrement tubs. We petitioned for a removal of the sick into the hospitals, but were denied. We remonstrated against the ungenerous usage of being confined with the privates, as being contrary to the laws and customs of nations, and particularly ungrateful in them, in consequence of the gentlemen-like usage which the British imprisoned officers met with in America; and thus we wearied ourselves petitioning and remonstrating, but to no purpose at all, for General Massey, who commanded at Halifax, was as inflexible as the Devil himself; (a fine preparative this for Mr. Lovel, member of the Continental Congress).

Lieut. Russel (whom I have mentioned before) came to visit me in prison, and assured me that he had done his utmost to procure my parole for enlargement; at which a British Captain, who was then the town-major, expressed compassion for the gentlemen confined in the filthy place, and assured me that he had used his influence to procure their enlargement; his name was near like Ramsay—Among the prisoners there were five in number, who had a legal claim to a parole, viz. James Lovel, Esqr. Capt. Francis Proctor, a Mr. Howland, master of a continental armed vessel, a Mr. Taylor, his mate and myself.

[66]

As to the article of provision, we were well served, much better than in any part of my captivity; and since it was Mr. Lovel's misfortune and mine to be prisoners, and in so wretched circumstances, I was happy that we were together, as a mutual support to each other, and to the unfortunate prisoners with us. Our first attention was the preservation of ourselves and injured little republic; the rest of our time we devoted interchangeably to politics and philosophy, as patience was a needful exercise in so evil a situation, but contentment mean and impracticable.

I had not been in this gaol many days, before a worthy and charitable woman, Mrs. Blacden by name, supplied me with a good dinner of fresh meats every day, with garden fruit, and sometimes with a bottle of wine; notwithstanding which I had not been more than three weeks in this place, before I lost all appetite to the most delicious food by the gaol distemper, as sundry of the prisoners, particularly a sergeant Moore, a man of courage and fidelity: I have several times seen him hold the boatswain of the Solebay frigate, when he attempted to strike him, and laughed him out of conceit of using him as a slave.

A doctor visited the sick, and did the best (as I suppose) he could for them, to no apparent purpose. I grew weaker and weaker, as did the rest, several of them could not help themselves. At last I reasoned in my own mind, that raw onion would be good: I made use of it, and found immediate relief by it, as did the sick in general, particularly sergeant Moore, who it recovered almost from the shades; though I had met with a little revival, still I found the malignant hand of Britain had greatly reduced my constitution with stroke upon stroke. Esquire Lovel and myself, used every argument and entreaty that could be well conceived of, in order to obtain gentleman-like usage, to no purpose. I then wrote Gen. Massey as severe a letter as I possibly could, with my friend Lovel's assistance: the contents of it was to give the British, as a nation, and him as an individual, their true character. This roused the rascal, for he could not bear to see his and the nation's deformity in that transparent letter, which I sent him; he therefore put himself in a great rage about it,

[68]

and shewed the letter to a number of British officers, particularly to Capt. Smith of the Lark frigate, who instead of joining with him in disapprobation, commended the spirit of it; upon which Gen. Massey said to him do you take the part of a rebel against me? Capt. Smith answered, that he rather spoke his sentiments, and there was a dissention in an opinion between them. Some officers took the part of the General, and others of the Captain: This I was informed of by a gentleman who had it from Capt. Smith.

In a few days after this the prisoners were ordered to go on board of a man of war, which was bound for New York; but two of them were not able to go on board, and were left at Halifax; one died, and the other recovered. This was about the 12th of October, and soon after we had got on board, the Captain sent for me in particular to come on the quarter deck: I went, not knowing that it was Capt. Smith, or his ship at that time, and expected to meet the same rigorous usage I had commonly met with, and prepared my mind accordingly; but when I came on deck, the Captain met me with his hand, welcomed me to his ship, invited me to

[69]

dine with him that day, and assured me that I should be treated as a gentleman, and that he had given orders, that I should be treated with respect by the ship's crew. This was so unexpected and sudden a transition, that it drew tears from my eyes, (which all the ill usage I had before met with, was not able to produce) nor could I at first hardly speak, but soon recovered myself, and expressed my gratitude for so unexpected a favour; and let him know, that I felt anxiety of mind in reflecting that his situation and mine was such, that it was not probable that it would ever be in my power to return the favour. Capt. Smith replied, that he had no reward in view, but only treated me as a gentleman ought to be treated; he said this is a mutable world, and one gentleman never knows but that it may be in his power to help another. Soon after I found this to be the same Capt. Smith who took my part against Gen. Massey; but he never mentioned any thing of it to me, and I thought it impolite in me to interrogate him, as to any disputes which might have arisen between him and the General on my account, as I was a prisoner, and that it was at his option to make free with me on that subject; if he pleased; and if he did not, I might take it for granted that it would be unpleasing for me to query about it, though I had a strong propensity to converse with him on that subject.

I dined with the Captain agreeable to his invitation, and oftentimes with the Lieutenants in the gun-room, but in general eat and drank with my friend Lovel, and the other gentlemen, who were prisoners with me, where I also slept.

We had a little birth enclosed with canvas, between decks, where we enjoyed ourselves very well, in hopes of an exchange; besides our friends at Halifax had a little notice of our departure, and supplied us with spirituous liquor, and many articles of provision for the coast. Capt. Burk having been taken prisoner, was added to our company (he had commanded an American armed vessel) and was generously treated by the Captain and all the officers of the ship, as well as myself. We now had in all near 30 prisoners on board, and as we were sailing along the coast, (if I recollect right) off Rhode Island, Capt. Burk with an under officer of the ship, (whose name I do not recollect) came to our little birth, proposed to kill Capt. Smith and the principal officers of the frigate and take it; adding that there was 35,000*l* sterling in the same. Capt. Burk likewise averred that a strong party out of the ship's crew, was in the conspiracy, and urged me and the gentlemen that was with me to use our influence with the private prisoners, to execute the design, and take the ship with the cash into one of our own ports.

Upon which I replied, that we had been too well used on board to murder the officers; that I could by no means reconcile it to my conscience, and that in fact it should not be done; and while I was yet speaking, my friend Lovel confirmed what I had said, and further pointed out the ungreatfulness of such an act; that it did not fall short of murder, and in fine all the gentlemen in the birth, opposed Captain Burk and his colleague: But they strenuously urged that the conspiracy would be found out, and that it would cost them their lives, provided they did not execute their design. I then interposed spiritedly, and put an end to further arguments on the subject, and told them that they might depend upon it, upon my honor, that I would

[72]

faithfully guard Captain Smith's life: if they should attempt the assault, I would assist him, (for they desired me to remain neuter) and that the same honor that guarded Captain Smith's life, would also guard theirs, and it was agreed by those present not to reveal the conspiracy, to the intent that no man should be put to death, in consequence of what had been projected, and Captain Burk and his colleague went to stifle the matter, among their associates. I could not help calling to mind what Captain Smith said to me, when I first came on board: "This is a mutable world, and one gentleman never knows but that it may be in his power to help another."—Captain Smith and his officers still behaved with their usual courtesy, I never heard any more of the conspiracy.

We arrived before New York, and cast anchor the latter part of October, where we remained several days, and where Captain Smith informed me, that he had recommended me to Adm. Howe and General Sir Wm. Howe, as a gentleman of honour and veracity, and desired I might be treated as such. Captain Burk was then ordered on board a prison ship in the harbor. I took my leave of Captain Smith, and with the other prisoners was sent on board a transport ship, which lay in the harbor, commanded by Capt. Craige, who took me into the cabin with him and his Lieut. I fared as they did, and was in every respect well treated in consequence of directions from Capt. Smith...In a few weeks after this I had the happiness to part with my friend Lovel, (for his sake, who the enemy affected to treat as a private, he was a gentleman of merit, and liberally educated, but had no commission, they malignantly treated him on account of his unshaken attachment to the cause of his country). He was exchanged for Gov. Phillip Skene of the British. I was continued in this ship till the latter part of November, where I contracted an acquaintance with the Captain of the British, (his name has slipped my memory). He was what we may call a genteel hearty fellow. I remember an expression of his over a bottle of wine, to this import: "That there is greatness of soul for personal friendship to subsist between you and me, as we are upon opposite sides, and may at another day be obliged to face each other in the field." (I am confident that he was as faithful as any officer in the British army). At another sitting he offered to bet a dozen of wine, that fort Washington would be in the hands of the British in three days. I stood the bet, (and would had I known that that would have been the case) and the third day afterwards we heard a prodigious heavy cannonade, and that day the fort was taken sure enough. Some months after, (when I was on parole) he called upon me with his usual humour, and mentioned the bet. I acknowledged I had lost it, but he said he did not mean to take it then, as I was a prisoner, that he would another day call on me, when their army came to Bennington. I replied that he was quite too generous, as I had fairly lost it, besides the Green Mountain Boys would not suffer them to come to Bennington. This was all in good humour, I should have been glad to have seen him after the defeat of Bennington, but did not...It was customary for the guard to attend the prisoners, which was often changed. One was composed of tories from Connecticut, in the vicinity of Fairfield and Green Farms. The sergeant's name was Hoit. They were very full of their invectives against the country, swaggered of their loyalty to their king, and exclaimed bitterly against the "cowardly yankees," (as they were pleased to term them) but finally contented themselves with saying, that when the country was overcome, they should be well rewarded for their loyalty, out of the estates of the whigs, which would be confiscated. This I found to be the general language of tories, after I arrived from England on the American coast. I heard sundry of them relate, that the British Generals had engaged them an ample reward for their losses, disappointments and expenditures, out of the forfeited rebel's estates.—This language early taught me what to do with tories estates, as far as my influence can go. For it is really a game of hazard between whig and tory. The whigs must inevitably have lost all, in consequence of the abilities of the tories, and their good friends the British; and it is no more than right the tories should run the same risque, in consequence of the abilities of the whigs, but of this more will be observed in the sequel of this narrative.

Some of the last days of November, the prisoners were landed at New-York, and I was admitted to parole with the other officers, viz. Proctor, Howland and Taylor. The privates were put into the filthy churches in New-York, with the distressed prisoners that were taken at fort Washington, and the second night sergeant Roger Moore (who was bold and enterprizing) found means to make his escape with every of the remaining prisoners that were taken with me, except three who were soon after exchanged: So that out of thirty-one prisoners, who went with me the round exhibited in these sheets, two only died with the enemy, and three only exchanged, one of whom died after he came within our lines, all the rest at different times, made their escape from the enemy.

I now found myself on parole, and restricted to the limits of the city of New York, where I soon projected means to live in some measure agreeable to my rank, though I was destitute of cash. My constitution was almost worn out by such a long and barbarous captivity. The enemy gave out that I was crazy, and wholly unmanned, but my vitals held sound, (nor was I delirious any more than I have been from my youth up, but my extreme circumstances at certain times, rendered it political to act in some measure the madman), and in consequence of a regular diet and exercise, my blood recruited, and my nerves in great measure recovered their former tone, strength and usefulness, in the course of six months.

I next invite the reader to a retrospect sight and consideration of the doleful scene of inhumanity exercised by Gen. Sir Wm. Howe, and the army under his command, towards the prisoners taken on Long Island, on the 27th day of August, 1776, sundry of whom were in an inhuman and barbarous manner, murdered after they had surrendered their arms, particularly a Gen. Odel, (or Woodhul) of the militia, who was hacked to pieces with cutlasses (when alive) by the light horsemen, and a Captain Fellows, of the Continental army, who was thrust through with a bayonet, of which wound he died instantly.

Sundry others were hanged up by the neck till they were dead, 5 on the limb of a white oak tree, and without any reason assigned, (except that they were fighting in defence of the only blessing worth preserving), and indeed those who had the misfortune to fall into their hands at fort Washington, in the month of November following, met with but very little better usage, except that they were reserved from immediate death to famish and die with hunger, in fine the word rebel applied to any vanquished persons, without regard to rank, who were in the continental service, on the 27th of August aforesaid, was thought (by the enemy) sufficient to sanctify whatever cruelties they were pleased to inflict death itself not excepted: but to pass over particulars which would swell my narrative far beyond my design.

The private soldiers who were brought to New York, were crowded into churches, and environed with slavish Hessian guards, a people of a strange language, who were sent to America for no other design but cruelty and desolation; and at others, by merciless Britons, whose mode of communicating ideas being intelligible in this country, served only to tantalize and insult the helpless and perishing; but above all the hellish delight and triumph of the tories over them, as they were dying by hundreds: This was too much for me to bear as a spectator; for I saw the tories exulting over the dead bodies of their murdered countrymen. I have gone into the churches, and seen sundry of the prisoners in the agonies of death, in consequence of very hunger, and others speechless and near death, biting pieces of chips; others pleading for God's sake, for something to eat, and at the same time shivering with the cold. Hollow groans saluted my ears, and despair seemed to be imprinted on every of their countenances. The filth of these churches (in consequence of the fluxes) was almost beyond description. The floors were covered with excrements, I have carefully sought to direct my steps so as to avoid it, but could not. They would beg for God's sake for one copper, or morsel of bread. I have seen in one of these churches seven dead at the same time, lying among the excrements of their bodies.

It was a common practice with the enemy, to convey the dead from these filthy places, in carts, to be slightly buried, and I have seen whole gangs of tories making derision, and exulting over the dead, saying there goes another load of damned rebels. I have observed the British soldiers to be full of their blackguard jokes, and

[80]

vaunting on those occasions, but they appeared to me less malignant than tories.

The provision dealt out to the prisoners was by no means sufficient for the support of life: it was deficient in quantity, and much more so in quality. The prisoners often presented me with a sample of their bread, which I certify was damaged to that degree, that it was loathsome and unfit to be eaten, and I am bold to aver it, (as my opinion) that it had been condemned, and was of the very worst sort. I have seen and been fed upon damaged bread, (in the course of my captivity) and observed the quality of such bread as has been condemned by the enemy, among which was very little so effectually spoiled as what was dealt out to these prisoners. Their allowance of meat (as they told me) was quite trifling, and of the basest sort, I never saw any of it, but was informed (bad as it was) it was swallowed almost as quick as they got hold of it. I saw some of them sucking bones after they were speechless; others who could yet speak, and had the use of their reason, urged me in the strongest and most pathetic manner, to use my interest in their behalf, for you plainly see (say they) that we are devoted to death and destruction; and after I had examined more particularly into their truly deplorable condition, and had become more fully apprized of the essential facts, I was persuaded that it was a premeditated and systematical plan of the British council, to destroy the youths of our land, with a view thereby to deter the country, and make it submit to their despotism; but that I could not do them any material service, and that by any public attempt for that purpose I might endanger myself by frequenting places the most nauseous and contagious that could be conceived of. I refrained going into the churches, but frequently conversed with such of the prisoners as were admitted to come out into the yard, and found that the systematical usage still continued. The guard would often drive me away with their fixed bayonets. A Hessian (one day) followed me five or six rods, but by making use of my legs, got rid of the lubber. Sometimes I could obtain a little conversation, notwithstanding their severities.

I was in one of the church yards, and it was rumoured among those in the church, and sundry of the prisoners came with their usual complaints to me, and among the rest a large boned tall young man, (as he told me from Pennsylvania) who was reduced to a mere skeleton; said he was glad to see me before he died, which he had expected to have done last night, but was a little revived; he furthermore informed me, that he and his brother had been urged to enlist in the British service, but had both resolved to die first; that his brother had died last night, in consequence of that resolution, and that he expected shortly to follow him; but I made the other prisoners stand a little off, and told him, with a low voice, to list; he then asked, whether it was right in the sight of God? I assured him that it was, and that duty to himself obliged him to deceive the British by enlisting, and deserting the first opportunity: upon which he answered with transport, that he would list. I charged him not to mention my name as his adviser, least it should get air, and I should be closely confined, in consequence of it. The integrity of these suffering prisoners is hardly credible. Many hundreds, I am confident, submitted to death, rather than enlist in the British service, which (I am informed) they most generally were pressed to do. I was astonished at the resolution of the two brothers particularly; it seems that they could not be stimulated to such exertions of heroism from ambition, as they were but obscure soldiers; strong indeed must the internal principle of virtue be, which supported them to brave death, and one of them went through the operation, as did many hundred others. I readily grant, that instances of public virtue are no excitement to the sordid and vicious, nor on the other hand, with all the barbarity of Britain and Heshland awaken them to a sense of their duty to the public; but these things will have their proper effect on the generous and brave . . . The officers on parole were most of them zealous, if possible, to afford the miserable soldiery relief, and often consulted, with one another on the subject, but to no effect, being destitute of the means of subsistence, which they needed; nor could the officers project any measure, which they thought would alter their fate, or so much as be a means of getting them out of those filthy places to the privilege of fresh air. Some projected that all the officers should go in procession to Gen. Howe, and plead the cause of the perishing soldiers;

but this proposal was negatived for the following reasons, viz. because that general Howe must needs be well acquainted and have a thorough knowledge of the state and condition of the prisoners in every of their wretched apartments, and that much more particular and exact than any officer on parole could be supposed to have, as the general had a return of the circumstances of the prisoners, by his own officers every morning, of the number which were alive, as also the number which died every 24 hours, and consequently the bill of mortality, as collected from the daily returns, lay before him with all the material situations and circumstances of the prisoners; and provided the officers should go in procession to gen. Howe, according to the projection, it would give him the greatest affront, and that he would either retort upon them; that it was no part of their parole to instruct him in his conduct to prisoners; that they were mutinying against his authority, and by affronting him, had forfeited their parole: or that more probably, instead of saying one word to them, would order them all into as wretched a confinement as the soldiers whom they sought to relieve; for

[85]

at that time, the British, from the general to the private centinel, were in full confidence, nor did they so much as hesitate but that they should conquer the country. Thus the consultation of the officers was confounded and broken to pieces, in consequence of the dread, which at that time lay on their minds, of offending gen. Howe; for they conceived so murderous a tyrant would not be too good to destroy even the officers, on the least pretence of an affront, as they were equally in his power with the soldiers; and as gen. Howe perfectly understood the condition of the private soldiers, it was argued that it was exactly such as he and his council had devised, and as he meant to destroy them it would be to no purpose for them to try to dissuade him from it, as they were helpless and liable to the same fate, on giving the least affront; indeed anxious apprehensions disturbed them in their then circumstances.

Mean time mortality raged to such an intolerable degree among the prisoners, that the very school boys in the streets knew the mental design of it in some measure, at least they knew that they were starved to death. Some poor

women contributed to their necessity, till their
children were almost starved, and all persons of
common understanding knew that they were
devoted to the cruelest and worst of deaths. It
was also proposed by some to make a written
representation of the condition of the soldiery,
and the officers to sign it, and that it should be
couched in such terms, as though they were apprehensive that the General was imposed upon
by his officers, in their daily returns to him of
the state and condition of the prisoners, and
that therefore the officers moved with compassion, were constrained to communicate to him
the facts relative to them, nothing doubting but
that they would meet with a speedy redress; but
this proposal was most generally negatived also,
and for much the same reason offered in the
other case, for it was conjectured that General
Howe's indignation would be moved against
such officers as should attempt to whip him over
his officers backs, that he would discern that
himself was really struck at, and not the officers,
who made the daily returns, and therefore self
preservation deterred the officers from either
petitioning or remonstrating to General Howe,

either verbally or in writing, as also the consideration that no valuable purpose to the distressed would be obtained.

I made several rough drafts on the subject, one of which I exhibited to Cols. Magaw, Miles and Atlee, and they said that they would consider the matter, soon after I called on them, and some of the gentlemen informed me, that they had wrote to the Gen. on the subject, and I concluded that the gentlemen thought it best that they should write without me, as there was such spirited aversion subsisting between the British and me.

In the mean time a Col. Hussecker, of the continental army, (as he then reported) was taken prisoner, and brought to New York, who gave out, that the country was most universally submitting to the English kings authority, and that there would be little or no opposition to Great Britain: This at first gave the officers a little shock, but in a few days they recovered themselves, for this Col. Hussecker, being a german, was feasting with Gen. D. Heister, his countryman, and from his conduct they were apprehensive, that he was a knave, at least he was

esteemed so by most of the officers, it was nevertheless a day of trouble. The enemy blasphemed,
our little army was retreating in New Jersey,
and our young men murdered by hundreds in
New York. The army of Britain and Heshland
prevailed for a little season, as though it was
ordered by Heaven to shew to the latest posterity, what the British would have done if they
could, and what the general calamity must have
been, in consequence of their conquering the
country, and to excite every honest man to stand
forth in the defence of liberty, and to establish
the independency of the United States of America forever, but this scene of adverse fortune
did not discourage a Washington, the illustrious American hero remained immovable. In
liberty's cause he took up his sword, this reflec-
tion was his support and consolation in the day
of his humiliation, when he retreated before the
enemy, through New Jersey into Pennsylvania.
Their triumph only roused his indignation, and
the important cause of his country, which lay
near his heart, moved him to cross the Delaware
again, and take ample satisfaction on his pursuers,
no sooner had he circumvallated his haughty

[89]

foes and appeared in *terible array*, but the host of Heshland fell. This taught America the intrinsic worth of perseverance, and the generous sons of freedom flew to the standard, of their common safeguard and defence, from which time the arm of American liberty hath prevailed.

This surprize and capture of the Hessians enraged the enemy, who were still vastly more numerous than the continental troops, they therefore collected, and marched from Princeton to attack General Washington, who was then at Trenton, having previously left a detachment from the main body at Princeton, for the support of that place. This was a trying time, for our worthy General (tho' in possession of a late most astonishing victory) was by no means able to withstand the collective force of the enemy, but his sagacity soon suggested a stratagem to effect that which by force to him was at that time impracticable, he therefore amused the enemy with a number of fires, and in the night made a forced march, undiscovered by them, and the next morning fell in with their rear guard at Princeton, and killed and took most of them prisoners, the main body too late perceiving their rear was attacked, hurried back with all speed, but to their mortification found they were out generaled, and baffled by General Washington, who was retired with his little army towards Morriston, and was out of their power. These repeated successes, one on the back of the other, chagrined the enemy prodigiously, and had an amazing operation in the scale of American politics, and undoubtedly was one of the corner stones, on which their fair structure of independency has been fabricated, for the country at no one time has ever been so much dispirited as just before the morning of this glorious success, which in part dispelled the gloomy clouds of oppression and slavery, which lay pending over America, big with the ruins of this and future generations, and enlightened and spirited her sons to redouble their blows on a merciless and haughty, and (I may add) perfidious enemy.

Furthermore this success had a mighty effect on Gen. Howe and his council, and roused them to a sense of their own weakness, and convinced them that they were neither omniscient or omnipotent, their obduracy and death designing malevolence in some measure, abated or was suspended. The prisoners who were condemned to the most wretched and cruelest of deaths and who survived to this period, (though most of them died before) were immediately ordered to be sent within General Washington's lines for an exchange, and in consequence of it, were taken out of their filthy and poisonous places of confinement, and sent out of New York to their friends in haste, several of them fell dead in the streets of New York, as they attempted to walk to the vessels in the harbour, for their intended embarkation... What numbers lived to reach the lines I cannot ascertain, but from concurrent representations which I have since received from numbers of people who lived in and adjacent to such parts of the country, where they were received from the enemy, I apprehend that most of them died in consequence of the vile usage of the enemy. Some who were eyewitnesses of that scene of mortality, (more especially in that part which continued after the exchange took place) are of opinion, that it was partly in consequence of a slow poison; but this I refer to the doctors that attended them, who are certainly the best judges.

Upon the best calculation I have been able to make from personal knowledge, and the many evidences I have collected in support of the facts, I learn that of the prisoners taken on Long Island, Fort Washington, and some few others, at different times and places, about 2000 perished with hunger, cold, and sickness occasioned by the filth of their prisons, at New York, and a number more on their passage to the continental lines; most of the residue who reached their friends, having received their death wound, could not be restored by the assistance of physicians and friends; but like their brother prisoners, fell a sacrifice to the relentless and scientific barbarity of Britain. I took as much pains as my circumstances would admit of, to inform myself not only of matters of fact, but likewise of the very designs and aims of Gen. Howe and his council; the latter of which I predicated on the former, and submit it to the candid public.

And lastly the aforesaid success of the American arms, had a happy effect on the continental officers, who were on parole at New York. A number of us assembled, but not in a public manner, and with full bowls and glasses, drank

Gen. Washington's health, and were not un-
mindful of Congress and our worthy friends on
the continent, and almost forgot that we were
prisoners.

A few days after this recreation, a British officer of rank and importance in their army,
(whose name I shall not mention in this narrative, for certain reasons, though I have mentioned it to some of my close friends and confidents) sent for me to his lodgings, and told me,
"That faithfulness, though in a wrong cause,
had nevertheless recommended me to General
Sir William Howe, who was minded to make me
a colonel of a regiment of new levies, (alias
tories) in the British service, and proposed that
I should go with him, and some other officers,
to England, who would embark for that purpose in a few days, and there be introduced to
Lord George Germaine, and probably to the
king; and that previously I should be cloathed
equal to such an introduction, and instead of
paper rags, be paid in hard guineas; after this I
should embark with General Burgoyne, and assist in the reduction of the country, which infal-
libly would be conquered, and when that should

be done, I should have a large tract of land, whether on the New Hampshire grants, or in Connecticut, it would make no odds, as the country would be forfeited to the crown." I then replied, "That if by faithfulness I had recommended myself to General Howe, I should be loth, by unfaithfulness, to lose the General's good opinion; besides that I viewed the offer of land to be similar to that which the devil offered Jesus Christ, "To give him all the kingdoms of the world, if he would fall down and worship him;" when at the same time the damned soul had not one foot of land upon earth. This closed the conversation, and the gentleman turned from me with an air of dislike, saying that I was a bigot, upon which I retired to my lodgings.

Near the last of November I was admitted to parole in New York, with many other American officers, and on the 22d day of January, 1777, was with them directed by the British commissary of prisoners, to be quartered on the westerly part of Long Island, and our parole continued. During my imprisonment there, no occurrences worth observation happened. I obtained the means of living as well as I desired, which in great measure repaired my constitution, which had been greatly injured by the severities of an inhuman captivity. I now began to feel myself composed, expecting either an exchange, or continuance in good and honourable treatment; but alas! my visionary expectations soon vanished. The news of the conquest of Ticonderoga by General Burgoyne, and the advance of his army into the country, made the haughty Britons again to feel their importance, and with that their insatiable thirst for cruelty.

The private prisoners at New York, and some of the officers on parole, felt the severity of it. Burgoyne was their toast and demigod; to him they paid adoration; in him the tories placed their confidence, "and forgot the Lord, their God," and served Howe, Burgoyne and Knyphausen,* "and became vile in their own imaginations, and their foolish hearts were darkened, professing" to be great politicians, and relying on foreign and merciless invaders, and with them seeking the ruin, bloodshed and destruction of their country, "became fools," expecting with them to share a dividend in the

* *Knyphausen, a Hessian general.*

confiscated estates of their neighbours and countrymen who fought for the whole country, and the religion and liberties thereof: "Therefore God gave them over to strong delusions, to believe a lie, that they all might be damned."

The 25th day of August I was apprehended, and under pretext of artful, mean and pitiful pretences; (that I had infringed on my parole) taken from a tavern, where there were more than a dozen officers present, and in the very place where those officers and myself were directed to be quartered, put under a strong guard, and taken to New York, where I expected to make my defence before the commanding officer; but contrary to my expectations, and without the least solid pretence of justice or a trial; was again encircled with a strong guard with fixed bayonets, and conducted to the provost-gaol in a lonely apartment, next above the dungeon, and was denied all manner of subsistence either by purchase or allowance. The second day I offered a guinea for a meal of victuals, but was denied it, and the third day I offered eight Spanish milled dollars for a like favour, but was denied, and all that I could get out of the sergeant's mouth, was, that by God he would obey his orders. I now perceived myself to be again in substantial trouble. In this condition I formed an oblique acquaintance with a Capt. Travis, of Virginia, (who was in the dungeon below me) through a little hole which was cut with a pen-knife, through the floor of my apartment, which communicated with the dungeon) it was a small crevice, through which I could discern but a very small part of his face at once, when he plied it to the hole; but from the discovery of him in the situation which we were both then in, I could not have known him, (which I found to be true by an after acquaintance). I could never-theless hold a conversation with him, and soon perceived him to be a gentleman of high spirits, who had a high sense of honor, and felt as big, as though he had been in a palace, and had treasures of wrath, in store against the British. In fine I was charmed with the spirit of the man; he had been near or quite four months in that dungeon, with murderers, thieves, and every species of criminals, and all for the sole crime of unshaken fidelity to his country; but his spirits were above dejection, and his mind unconquerable. I engaged to do him every service in my power, and in a few weeks afterwards, with the united petitions of the officers in the provost, procured his dismission from the dark mansion of fiends to the apartments of his petitioners.

And it came to pass on the 3d day, at the going down of the sun, that I was presented with a piece of boiled pork, and some biscuit, which the sergeant gave me to understand, was my allowance, and I fed sweetly on the same; but I indulged my appetite by degrees, and in a few days more, was taken from that apartment, and conducted to the next loft or story, where there was above 20 continental and some militia officers who had been taken and imprisoned there, besides some private gentlemen who had been dragged from their own homes to that filthy place, by tories. Several of every denomination mentioned died there, some before, and others after I was put there.

The history of the proceedings relative to the provost only, was I particular, would swell a volume larger than this whole narrative; I shall therefore only notice such of the occurrences which are most extraordinary.

Capt. Vandyke bore with an uncommon fortitude near 20 months confinement in this place, and in the mean time was very serviceable to others who were confined with him. The allegation against him, as the cause of his confinement, was very extraordinary: He was accused of setting fire to the city of New York, (at the time the west part of it was consumed) when it was a known fact, that he had been in the provost a week before the fire broke out; and in like manner, frivolous were the ostensible accusations against most of those who were there confined; the case of two militia officers excepted, who were taken in their attempting to escape from their parole; and probably there may be some other instances which might justify such a confinement.

Mr. William Miller, a committee man, from West Chester county, and State of New York, was taken from his bed in the dead of night, by his tory neighbours, and was starved for three days and nights in a department of the same gaol; add to this the denial of fire, and that in a cold season of the year, in which time he walked day and night, to defend himself against the

[100]

frost, and when he complained of such reprehensible conduct, the word rebel or committee man was deemed by the enemy a sufficient atonement for any inhumanity that they could invent or inflict. He was a man of good natural understanding, a close and sincere friend to the liberties of America, and endured 14 months cruel imprisonment with that magnanimity of soul, which reflects honor on himself and country.

Major Levi Wells and Capt. Ozias Bissel were apprehended and taken under guard from their parole on Long Island, to the provost, on as fallacious pretences as the former, and were there continued till their exchange took place, which was near 5 months. Their fidelity and zealous attachment to their country's cause, which was more than commonly conspicuous was undoubtedly the real cause of their confinement.

Major Brinton Payne, Capt. Flahaven, and Capt. Randolph, who had at different times distinguished themselves by their bravery, especially as the several actions in which they were taken, was all the provocation they gave, for which they suffered about a years confinement each in the same filthy gaol.

A few weeks after my confinement, on the like fallacious and wicked pretences, was brought to the same place, from his parole on Long Island, Major Otho Holland Williams, (now a full Colonel in the continental army). In his character are united the gentleman, officer, soldier, and friend; he walked through the prison with an air of great disdain; said he, "Is this the treatment which gentlemen of the continental army are to expect from the rascally British, when in their power? Heavens forbid it!" He was continued there about five months, and then exchanged for a British Major.

John Fell, Esqr. (now a member of Congress for the state of New Jersey) was taken from his own house by a gang of infamous tories, and by order of a British General was sent to the provost, where he was continued near one year. The stench of the gaol, which was very loathsome and unhealthy, occasioned a hoarseness of the lungs, which proved fatal to many who were there confined, and reduced this gentleman near to the point of death; he was indeed given over by his friends who were about him, and himself concluded he must die. I could not endure the thought that so worthy a friend to America should have his life stole from him in such a mean, base, and scandalous manner, and that his family and friends should be bereaved of so great and desirable a blessing, as his further care, usefulness and examples, might prove to them. I therefore wrote a letter to Gen. Robertson, (who commanded in town) and being touched with the most sensible feelings of humanity, which dictated my pen to paint dying distress in such lively colours that it wrought conviction even on the obduracy of a British General, and produced his order to remove the now honourable John Fell, Esqr. out of gaol, to private lodgings in town; in consequence of which he slowly recovered his health. There is so extraordinary a circumstance which intervened, concerning this letter, that it is worth noticing.

Previous to the sending it, I exhibited the same to the gentlemen on whose behalf it was wrote, for his approbation, and he forbid me to send it in the most positive and explicit terms; his reason was, "That the enemy knew by every morning's report the condition of all the prisoners, mine in particular, as I have been gradually coming to my end for a considerable time, and they very well knew it, and likewise determined it should be accomplished, as they had served many others; that to ask a favor, would give the merciless enemy occasion to triumph over me in my last moments, and therefore I will ask no favors from them, but resign myself to my supposed fate." But the letter I sent without his knowledge, and I confess I had but little expectations from it, yet could not be easy till I had sent it. It may be worth a remark, that this gentleman was an Englishman born, and from the beginning of the revolution, has invariably asserted, and maintained the cause of liberty.

The British have made so extensive an improvement of the provost during the present revolution until of late, that a very short definition will be sufficient for the dullest apprehensions. It may be with propriety called the British inquisition, and calculated to support their oppressive measures and designs, by suppressing the spirit of liberty; as also a place to confine the criminals, and most infamous wretches of their own army, where many gentlemen of the American army, and citizens thereof, were promiscuously confined, with every species of criminals; but they divided into different apartments, and kept at as great a remove as circumstances permitted, but it was nevertheless at the option of a villainous sergeant who had the charge of the provost, to take any gentleman from their room, and put them into the dungeon, which was often the case: At two different times I was taken down stairs for that purpose, by a file of soldiers with fixed bayonets, and the sergeant brandishing his sword at the same time, and having been brought to the door of the dungeon, I there flattered the vanity of the sergeant, whose name was Keef, by which means I procured the surprising favour to return to my companions; but some of the high mettled young gentlemen could not bear his insolence, and determined to keep at a distance, and neither please or displease the villain, but none could keep clear of his abuse; however mild measures were the best; he did not hesitate to call us damned rebels, and use us with the coarsest language. The capts. Flahaven, Randolph and Mercer, were the objects of his most flagrant and repeated abuses, who were many times taken to the dungeon, and there continued at his pleasure. Capt. Flahaven took cold in the dungeon, and was in a declining state of health, but an exchange delivered him, and in all probability saved his life...It was very mortifying to bear with the insolence of such a vicious and ill bred imperious rascal. Remonstrances against him were preferred to the commander of the town, but no relief could be obtained, for his superiors were undoubtedly well pleased with his abusive conduct to the gentlemen, under the severities of his power; and remonstrating against his infernal conduct only served to confirm him in authority, and for this reason I never made any remonstrances on the subject, but only stroaked him, for I knew that he was but a cat's paw in the hands of the British officers, and that if he should use us well, he would immediately be put out of that trust, and a worse man appointed to succeed him; but there was no need of making any new appointment, for Cunningham, their provost marshal, and Keef, his deputy, were as great rascals as their army could boast of, except one Joshua Loring, an infamous tory, who was commissary of prisoners, nor can any of these be supposed to be equally criminal with gen. Sir William Howe and his associates, who prescribed and directed the murders and cruelties, which were by them perpetrated. This Loring is a monster!...There is not his like in human shape: He exhibits a smiling countenance, seems to wear a phiz of humanity, but has been instrumentally capable of the most consummate acts of wickedness, (which were firstly projected by an abandoned British council, cloathed with the authority of a Howe) murdering premeditately (in cold blood) near or quite 2000 helpless prisoners, and that in the most clandestine, mean and shameful manner, (at N. York.) He is the most mean spirited, cowardly, deceitful, and destructive animal in God's creation below, and legions of infernal devils, with all their tremendous horrors, are impatiently ready to receive Howe and him, with all their detestable accomplices, into the most exquisite agonies of the hottest regions of hell fire.

The sixth day of July, 1777, gen. St. Clair and the army under his command, evacuated Ticonderoga, and retreated with the main body through Hubbardton into Castleton, which was but six miles distance, when his rear guard commanded by col. Seth Warner, was attacked at Hubbardton by a body of the enemy of about 2000 commanded by gen. Fraser. Warner's command consisted of his own and two other regiments, viz. Francis's, and Hale's and some scattering and enfeebled soldiers. His whole number, according to information, was near or quite 1000; part of which were Green Mountain Boys; about 700 out of the whole he brought into action. The enemy advanced boldly, and the two bodies formed within about sixty yards of each other. Col. Warner having formed his own regiment, and that of col. Francis's, did not wait for the enemy, but gave them a heavy fire from his whole line, and they returned it with great bravery. It was by this time dangerous for those of both parties, who were not prepared for the world to come; but col. Hale being apprised of the danger, never brought his regiment to the charge, but left Warner and Francis to stand the blowing of it, and fled, but luckily fell in with an inconsiderable number of the enemy, and to his eternal shame, surrendered himself a prisoner.

The conflict was very bloody. Col. Francis fell in the same, but col. Warner, and the officers

[108]

under his command, as also the soldiery, behaved with great resolution. The enemy broke, and gave way on the right and left, but formed again, and renewed the attack; in the mean time the British grenadiers, in the centre of the enemy's line, maintained the ground, and finally carried it with the point of the bayonet, and Warner retreated with reluctance. Our loss was about 30 men killed, and that of the enemy amounting to 300 killed, including a major Grant. The enemy's loss I learnt from the confession of their own officers, when a prisoner with them. I heard them likewise complain, that the Green Mountain Boys took sight. The next movement of the enemy, of any material consequence, was their investing Bennington, (with a design to demolish it, and subject its Mountaineers, to which they had a great aversion), with 1500 chosen men, including tories, with the highest expectation of success, and having chosen an eminence of strong ground, fortified it with slight breast works, and two pieces of cannon; but the government of the young state of Vermont, being previously jealous of such an attempt of the enemy, and in due time had pro-

[109]

cured a number of brave militia from the government of the state of New Hampshire, who together with the militia of the north part of Berkshire county, and state of Massachusett's, and the Green Mountain Boys, constituted a body of desperadoes, under the command of the intrepid gen. Stark, who in number were about equal to the enemy. Col. Herrick, who commanded the Green Mountain Rangers, and who was second in command, being thoroughly acquainted with the ground where the enemy had fortified, proposed to attack them in their works, upon all parts at the same time. This plan being adopted by the general and his council of war, the little militia brigade of undisciplined heroes, with their long brown firelocks, (the best security of a free people) without either cannon or bayonets, was, on the 16th day of August, led on to the attack by their bold commanders, in the face of the enemy's dreadful fire, (and to the astonishment of the world, and burlesque of discipline) carried every part of their lines in less than one quarter of an hour after the attack became general, took their cannon, killed and captivated more than two thirds of their number, which immortalized gen. Stark, and made Bennington famous to posterity.

Among the enemy's slain was found Col. Baum, their commander, a Col. Pfester, who headed an infamous gang of tories, and a large part of his command, and among the prisoners was Major Meibome, their second in command, a number of British and Hessian officers, surgeons, &c. and more than one hundred of the aforementioned Pfester's command. The prisoners being collected together, were sent to the meeting house in the town, by a strong guard, and General Stark not imagining any present danger, the militia scattered from him to rest and refresh themselves, in this situation he was on a sudden attacked by a reinforcement of 1,100 of the enemy, commanded by Gov. Skene, with two field pieces, they advanced in regular order, and kept up the incessant fire, especially from their field pieces, and the remaining militia retreating slowly before them, disputed the ground inch by inch. The enemy were heard to halloo to them, saying stop Yankees... In the mean time Col. Warner, with about 130 men of his regiment, (who were not in the first action) ar-

[111]

rived and attacked the enemy with great fury, (being determined to have ample revenge on account of the quarrel at Hubbardton) which brought them to a stand, and soon after Gen. Stark and Col. Herrick brought on more of the scattered militia and the action became general, in a few minutes the enemy were forced from their cannon, gave way on all parts and fled, and the shouts of victory were a second time proclaimed in favour of the militia. The enemy's loss in killed and prisoners, in these two actions, amounted to more than 1200 men, and our loss did not exceed 50 men...This was a bitter stroke to the enemy, but their pride would not permit them to hesitate but that they could vanquish the country, and as a specimen of their arrogancy, I shall insert general Burgoyne's Proclamation.

Proclamation:

"*By John Burgoyne, Esq. Lieutenant General of his Majesty's armies in America, Colonel of the Queen's regiment of light dragoons, Governor of fort William in North Britain, one of the Representatives of the Commons of Great Britain in Parliament, and commanding an army, and fleet employed on an expedition from Canada, &c. &c. &c.*

[112]

"The forces entrusted to my command are designed to act in concert and upon a common principal, with the numerous armies and fleets which already display in every quarter of America, the power, the justice, and when properly sought, the mercy of the king.

"The cause in which the British arms are thus exerted, applies to the most affecting interests of the human heart, and the military servants of the crown, at first called forth for the sole purpose of restoring the rights of the constitution, now combine with love of their country, and duty to their sovereign, the other extensive incitements which spring from a due sense of the general privileges of mankind. To the eyes and ears of the temperate part of the public, and to the breasts of suffering thousands in the provinces, be the melancholy appeal, whether the present unnatural rebellion has not been made a foundation for the completest system of tyranny that ever God in his displeasure, suffered for a time to be exercised over a froward and stubborn generation.

"Arbitrary imprisonment, confiscation of property, persecution and torture, unprecedented in the inquisitions of the Romish church, are among the palpable enormities that verify the affirmative. These are inflicted by assemblies and committees, who dare to profess themselves friends to liberty, upon the most quiet subjects, without distinction of age or sex, for the sole crime, often for the sole suspicion, of having adhered in principal to the government under which they were born, and to which by every tie, divine and human, they owe allegiance. To consummate these shocking proceedings, the profanation of religion is added to the most profligate prostitution of common reason, the consciences of men are set at nought, and multitudes are compelled not only to bear arms, but also to swear subjection to an usurpation they abhor.

"Animated by these considerations, at the head of troops in the full powers of health, discipline, and valor, determined to strike where necessary, and anxious to spare where possible, I by these presents invite and exhort all persons, in all places where the progress of this army may point ... and by the blessing of God I will extend if far ... to maintain such conduct as may justify me in protecting their lands, habitations,

[114]

and families. The intention of this address is to hold forth security, not depredation to the country... To those whom spirit and principle may induce to partake the glorious task of redeeming their countrymen from dungeons, re-establishing the blessings of a legal government, I offer encouragement and employment, and upon the first intelligence of their associations, I will find means to assist their undertakings. The domestic, the industrious, the infirm, and even the timid inhabitants, I am desirous to protect, provided they remain quietly at their houses, that they do not suffer their cattle to be removed, nor their corn or farage to be secreted or destroyed, that they do not break up their bridges or roads, nor by any other act, directly or indirectly, endeavor to obstruct the operations of the king's troops, or supply or assist those of the enemy... Every species of provision brought to my camp, will be paid for at an equitable rate, and in solid coin.

"In consciousness of christianity, my royal master's clemency and the honor of soldiership, I have dwelt upon this invitation, and wished for more persuasive terms to give it impression:

[115]

And let not people be led to disregard it, by considering their distance from the immediate situation of my camp...I have but to give stretch to the Indian forces under my direction, and they amount to thousands, to overtake the hardened enemies of Great Britain and America: I consider them the same wherever they may lurk.

"If notwithstanding these endeavours, and sincere inclinations to effect them, the phrensy of hostility should remain, I trust I shall stand acquitted in the eyes of God and men, in denouncing and executing the vengeance of the state against the wilful outcasts. The messengers of justice and of wrath await them in the field; and devastation, famine, and every concomitant horror that a reluctant but indispensible prosecution of military duty must occasion, will bar the way to their return.

J. BURGOYNE.

"Camp near Ticonderoga, 4th, July 1777.

"By order of his Excellency the Lieut. General.

ROBERT KINGSTON, Sectry."

Gen. Burgoyne was still the toast, and the severities towards the prisoners were in a great measure increased or diminished, in proportion to the expectation of conquest. His very ostentatious proclamation was in the hand and mouth of most of the soldiery, especially the tories, and from it, their faith was raised to assurance.... I wish my countrymen in general could but have an idea of the assuming tyranny, and haughty, malevolent, and insolent behaviour of the enemy at that time; and from thence discern the intolerable calamities which this country have extricated themselves from by their public spiritedness and bravery. The downfall of general Burgoyne, and surrender of his whole army, dashed the aspiring hopes and expectations of the enemy, and brought low the imperious spirit of an opulent, puissant and haughty nation, and made the tories bite the ground with anguish, exalting the valour of the free-born sons of America, and raised their fame and that of their brave commanders to the clouds, and immortalized gen. Gates with laurels of eternal duration. No sooner had the knowledge of this interesting and mighty event reached His Most Christian

Majesty, who in Europe shine with a superior lustre in goodness, policy and arms, but the illustrious potentate, auspiciously influenced by Heaven to promote the reciprocal interest and happiness of the ancient kingdom of France, and the new and rising states of America, passed the great and decisive decree, that the United States of America, should be free and independent. Vaunt no more old England! consider you are but an island! and that your power has been continued longer than the exercise of your humanity. Order your broken and vanquished battalions to retire from America, the scene of your cruelties. Go home and repent in dust and sackcloth for your aggravated crimes. The cries of bereaved parents, widows, and orphans, reach the heavens, and you are abominated by every friend to America. Take your friends the tories with you, and be gone, and drink deep of the cup of humiliation. Make peace with the princes of the house of Bourbon, for you are in no condition to wage war with them. Your veteran soldiers are fallen in America, and your glory is departed. Be quiet and pay your debts, especially for the hire of the Hessians. There is no other way for you to get into credit again, but by reformation and plain honesty, which you have despised; for your power is by no means sufficient to support your vanity. I have had opportunity to see a great deal of it, and felt its severe effects, and learned lessons of wisdom and policy, when I wore your heavy irons, and bore your bitter revilings and reproaches. I have something of a smattering of philosophy, and understand human nature in all its stages tolerably well; am thoroughly acquainted with your national crimes, and assure you that they not only cry aloud for Heaven's vengeance, but excite mankind to rise up against you. Virtue, wisdom and policy, are in a national sense always connected with power, or in other words, power is their offspring, and such power as is not directed by virtue, wisdom and policy, never fails finally to destroy itself as yours has done...It is so in the nature of things, and unfit it should be otherwise; for if it was not so, vanity, injustice, and oppression, might reign triumphant for ever. I know you have individuals, who still retain their virtue, and consequently their honor and humanity. Those I really pity, as they must more

[119]

or less suffer in the calamity, in which the nation plunged headlong; but as a nation I hate and despise you.

My affections are frenchified ... I glory in Louis the sixteenth, the generous and powerful ally of these states; am fond of a connection with so enterprising, learned, polite, courteous, and commercial a nation, and am sure that I express the sentiments and feelings of all the friends to the present revolution. I begin to learn the French tongue, and recommend it to my countrymen before Hebrew, Greek or Latin, (provided but one of them only are to be attended to) for the trade and commerce of these states in future must inevitably shift its channel from England to France, Spain, and Portugal; and therefore the statesman, politician and merchant need be acquainted with their several languages, particularly the French, which is much in vogue in most parts of Europe. Nothing could have served so effectually to illuminate, polish, and enrich these states as the present revolution, as well as preserve their liberty. Mankind are naturally too national, even to the degree of bigotry, and commercial intercourse with foreign nations has a great and necessary tendency, to improve mankind, and erase the superstition of the mind by acquainting them that human nature, policy and interest, are the same in all nations, and at the same time they are bartering commodities for the conveniences and happiness of each nation, they may reciprocally exchange such part of their customs and manners as may be beneficial, and learn to extend charity and good will to the whole world of mankind.

I was confined in the provost gaol at New York the 26th day of August, and continued there to the third day of May, 1778, when I was taken out under guard, and conducted to a sloop in the harbour at New York, in which I was guarded to Staten Island, to general Campbell's quarters, where I was admitted to eat and drink with the gen. and several other of the British field officers, and treated for two days in a polite manner. As I was drinking wine with them one evening, I made an observation on my transition from the provost criminals to the company of gentlemen, adding that I was the same man still, and should give the British credit by him, (speaking to the gen.) for two days good usage.

[121]

The next day col. Archibald Campbell (who was exchanged for me) came to this place, (conducted by Mr. Boudinot, the then American commissary of prisoners) and saluted me in a handsome manner, saying that he never was more glad to see any gentleman in his life, and I gave him to understand that I was equally glad to see him, and was apprehensive that it was from the same motive. The gentlemen present laughed at the fancy, and conjectured that sweet liberty was the foundation of our gladness; so we took a glass of wine together, and then I was accompanied by gen. Campbell, col. Campbell, Mr. Boudinot, and a number of British officers, to the boat, which was ready to sail to Elizabeth-town-point. Mean while I entertained them with a rehearsal of the cruelties exercised towards our prisoners; and assured them that I should use my influence, that their prisoners should be treated in future in the same manner, as they should in future treat ours; that I thought it was right in such extreme cases, that their example should be applied to their own prisoners; then exchanged the decent ceremonies of compliment, and parted: I sailed to the point aforesaid, and

" . . . *and saluted me . . . saying that he never was*
more glad to see any gentleman in his life."

in a transport of joy, landed on liberty ground, and as I advanced into the country, received the acclamations of a grateful people.

I soon fell into company with col. Sheldon, (of the light horse) who in a polite and obliging manner, accompanied me to headquarters, Valley Forge, where I was courteously received by gen. Washington, with peculiar marks of his approbation and esteem, and was introduced to most of the generals and many of the principal officers, of the army, who treated me with respect, and after having offered Gen. Washington my further service, in behalf of my country, as soon as my health (which was very much impaired) would admit, and obtain his license to return home, I took my leave of his excellency, and set out from Valley Forge with gen. Gates and his suit for Fish Kill, where we arrived the latter end of May. In this tour the gen. was pleased to treat me with the familiarity of a companion, and generosity of a lord, and to him I made known some striking circumstances which occurred in the course of my captivity. I then bid farewell to my noble gen. and the gentlemen of his retinue, and set out for Bennington, the

[123]

capital of the Green Mountain Boys, where I arrived the evening of the last day of May to their great surprise; for I was to them as one rose from the dead and now both their joy and mine was complete. Three cannon were fired that evening, and next morning col. Herrick gave orders, and fourteen more were discharged, welcoming me to Bennington, my usual place of abode; thirteen for the United States, and one for young Vermont.

After this ceremony was ended we moved the flowing bowl, and rural felicity, sweetened with friendship, glowed in each countenance, and with loyal healths to the rising states of America, concluded that evening, and with the same loyal spirit, I now conclude my Narrative.

A BIBLIOGRAPHY OF
THE WRITINGS OF ETHAN ALLEN

A BIBLIOGRAPHY OF
THE WRITINGS OF ETHAN ALLEN

A brief / Narrative / of the Proceedings / of the Government of / New-York, / relative to their obtaining the jurisdiction of / that / Large District of Land / to the Westward from / Connecticut River etc.

Bennington, 23d September, 1774.

Hartford: Printed by Eben Watson, near the Great Bridge.

The / Proceedings / of the / Convention / of the Representatives of the / New-Hampshire Settlers; / Containing / their Covenant-Compact and Resolutions; / And Also / Twelve Acts of OUTLAWRY, / Passed by the Legislature of the Province of NEW-YORK / against those Settlers, and their ANSWER to the / same. / Hartford: / Printed by Ebenezer Watson, near the Great-Bridge. 1775.

(The Library of Congress and the library of James B. Wilbur, Manchester, Vt. contain copies of this pamphlet signed, on the title page by Ethan Allen and others.)

An / Animadversory / Address / to the / Inhabitants / of the / State of Vermont; / with / Remarks on a Proclamation, under the Hand of / his Excellency George Clinton Esq; Governor / of the State of New-York.

Hartford: / Printed by Watson and Goodwin, near the Great Bridge. / MDCCLXXVIII.

(A copy inscribed in Ethan Allen's hand: "To be delivered to the Hon'ble. Brig. Genl. Stark.")

[127]

A / Vindication / of the Opposition of the Inhabitants / of / Vermont / to the Government of / New-York, / And of their Right to form an Independent / State. / Humbly submitted to the Consideration of the impar- / tial WORLD.

Printed by Alden Spooner, 1779, / Printer to the State of *Vermont.*

A / Narrative / of / Colonel Ethan Allen's / Captivity / ... Containing / His / Voyages and Travels ... Interspersed with some Political Observations / Written by himself, and now published for the Information of the / Curious in all Nations. / Price Ten Paper Dollars. / Philadelphia: / Printed and Sold by Robert Bell, in Third Street. / MDCCLXXIX.

(The Same) Philadelphia; Printed, / Boston: Re-printed. / Draper and Folsom, at their Printing / Office, at the Corner of Winter Street. / MDCCLXXIX.

(The Same originally appeared in weekly parts in the 'Pennsylvania Packet or General Advertiser' commencing with the number of November 9th, 1779, from which it was copied in other weekly newspapers of the country.)

(Many editions of the book followed. *See page* 133)

The / Present State / of the / Controversy / between / The States / of / New-York / and / New Hampshire / on the one part, / And the State / of / Vermont / on the other.

Hartford: / Printed by Hudson & Goodwin / MDCCLXXXII.

Reason / the only / Oracle of Man, / or a / Compenduous System / of / *Natural* Religion. / Alternately ADORNED with Confutations / of a variety of DOCTRINES / incom-

[128]

patible to it; / Deduced from the most exalted Ideas which / we are able to form of the / Divine and Human / Characters, / and from the /Universe in General./ Bennington:/ State of Vermont; / *Printed by* Haswell & Russell. / M,DCC,LXXXIX.

(There are several later editions.)

(A copy, in the possession of Prof. J. E. Goodrich, inscribed, in Ethan Allen's hand: "This Book is a present from the Author to his Lady.

> Dear Fanny wise, the beautiful and young,
> The partner of my Joys, my dearest self.
> My love, pride of my life, your Sexes pride
> And partner of sincere politeness,
> To thee a welcome compliment I make
> Of Treasures rich, the Oracles of Reason.")

A / Concise Refutation / of the / Claims / of / *New-Hampshire* and *Massachusetts-bay*, / to the Territory of / Vermont; / with / Occasional REMARKS on the long disputed / Claim of New-York to the same. / written by / *Ethan Allen* and *Jonas Fay*, Esq'rs. / And published by Order of the GOVERNOR and / COUNCIL of VERMONT. / BENNINGTON, the first Day of *January*, 1780. / Joseph Fay, Sec'ry. / Hartford: / Printed by Hudson and Goodwin.

(A letter addressed 'To the Inhabitants of the State of Vermont' and signed 'Ethan Allen. Arlington, 9th Jan. 1779' subjoined to) A / Vindication / of the Conduct of the / General Assembly / of the State of / Vermont, etc. / By Ira Allen. / Arlington, 9th Jan. 1779. / Dresden: / Printed by Alden Spooner.

[129]

(The following articles by Ethan Allen appeared in the Connecticut Courant, a weekly newspaper published at Hartford.)

(The most complete file of the Connecticut Courant—from which this collation was made—is contained in the Library of the Connecticut Historical Society, Hartford, Connecticut.)

Oct. 27, 1772. An answer to a letter from Governor Tryon, addressed 'To the Inhabitants of Bennington, and the adjacent Country' and dated Albany, 11th of August, 1772. (Signed.)

June 2, 1772. ' . . a true Narrative of the Sufferings and Abuses, received by Mr. Remember Baker, his Wife and Family, on the 22nd Day of March, A.D. 1772.' (Unsigned.)

July 7th, 1772. An answer to a letter from Governor Tryon addressed 'To the Reverend Mr. Dewey, and the Inhabitants of Bennington, and the adjacent Country on the East Side of Hudson's River' and dated New York 19th May, 1772. (Written by Allen but signed Ethan Allen, Seth Warner, Remember Baker, Robert Cockran.)

May 25, 1773. Advertisement of '*Ethan Allen* and Company.'

June 28, 1774. 'Supplement to the Connecticut Courant., Remarks, etc. on some late Laws passed in New-York.' (Written by Allen and signed Ethan Allen, Seth Warner, Remember Baker, Robert Cockran, Peleg Sunderland, John Smith, Salvanus Brown. Bennington April 15th, 1774.)

[130]

June 21, 1774. Supplement to the Connecticut Courant. Report of 'a general Meeting of the Committees for the several Townships on the West side of the Range of Green Mountains, . . . held at the House of Mr. Eliakim Wellers in Manchester, on the 1st Day of March A.D. 1774 etc.' (Written by Allen. 'Certified, pr Nathan Clark, Chairman. Jonas Fay, Clerk. Dated, Bennington, April 14th, 1774.')

Feb. 2, 1779. An answer to 'A Proclamation from his Excellency George Clinton Esq; Governor of the State of New-York' which appeared in the Connecticut Courant. (Signed Ethan Allen. Bennington, December 28, 1778.)

J. P.

A
LIST OF EDITIONS
OF ETHAN ALLEN'S NARRATIVE

1 – 1779, Philadelphia —Printed by Robert Bell. Double Columns.

2 – 1779, Boston —Reprint by Draper & Folsom. 40 Pages.

3 – 1779, Philadelphia —Sometimes called 1st Edition. Printed by Robert Bell. Single Columns.

4 – 1779, Boston —Reprint by Draper & Folsom.

5 – 1779, Philadelphia —Printed for and sold by William Mentz in Cherry Valley.

6 – 1780, Newbury, Mass. —Printed by John Mycoll for Nathaniel Coverly of Boston 80 Pages.

7 – 1780, Norwich, Conn. —Printed by John Trumbull.

8 – 1780, Danvers, near
  Salem, Mass. —Reprinted & sold by E. Russell.

9 – 1805, Philadelphia —Printed for Ira Allen of Vermont as an Appendix to the PARTICULARS OF THE CAPTURE OF THE SHIP OLIVE BRANCH.

10 – 1807, Walpole, N. H. —Printed by Charter & Hale for Thomas & Thomas. 158 pages.

11 – 1814, Albany, N. Y. —Printed by Moses Pratt, Jr., for Pratt & Clark.

12 – 1834, Plattsburgh, N.Y.—Printed by F. P. Allen for O.R. Cook. Slightly abridged copy of the "Narrative" in "Memoir of Colonel Ethan Allen" by Hugh Moore.

13 – 1838, Burlington, Vt. —Printed by H. Johnson & Co. Called 3rd Edition.

14 – 1845, Boston —Printed by Oliver L. Perkins.

15 – 1846, Burlington —Printed by Chauncey Goodrich. Called 4th Edition.

16 – 1849, Burlington —Printed by C. Goodrich & S. B. Nichols. Called 5th Edition.

17 – 1849, Dayton, Ohio —

18 – 1852, Burlington —Reprint of 16th (1849) edition Nichols & Warren, Leavenworth Block.

19 – 1854, Burlington —Reprint of 16th (1849) edition by Chauncey Goodrich.

20 – 1930, New York —Printed for the Ft. Ticonderoga Museum, by Richard W. Ellis: The Georgian Press, Westport, Ct., in an edition of 540 copies. Introduction by John Pell.

A CATALOG OF SELECTED
DOVER BOOKS
IN ALL FIELDS OF INTEREST

A CATALOG OF SELECTED DOVER
BOOKS IN ALL FIELDS OF INTEREST

100 BEST-LOVED POEMS, Edited by Philip Smith. "The Passionate Shepherd to His Love," "Shall I compare thee to a summer's day?" "Death, be not proud," "The Raven," "The Road Not Taken," plus works by Blake, Wordsworth, Byron, Shelley, Keats, many others. 96pp. 5⅜ x 8¼. 0-486-28553-7

100 SMALL HOUSES OF THE THIRTIES, Brown-Blodgett Company. Exterior photographs and floor plans for 100 charming structures. Illustrations of models accompanied by descriptions of interiors, color schemes, closet space, and other amenities. 200 illustrations. 112pp. 8⅜ x 11. 0-486-44131-8

1000 TURN-OF-THE-CENTURY HOUSES: With Illustrations and Floor Plans, Herbert C. Chivers. Reproduced from a rare edition, this showcase of homes ranges from cottages and bungalows to sprawling mansions. Each house is meticulously illustrated and accompanied by complete floor plans. 256pp. 9⅜ x 12¼.
0-486-45596-3

101 GREAT AMERICAN POEMS, Edited by The American Poetry & Literacy Project. Rich treasury of verse from the 19th and 20th centuries includes works by Edgar Allan Poe, Robert Frost, Walt Whitman, Langston Hughes, Emily Dickinson, T. S. Eliot, other notables. 96pp. 5⅜ x 8¼. 0-486-40158-8

101 GREAT SAMURAI PRINTS, Utagawa Kuniyoshi. Kuniyoshi was a master of the warrior woodblock print — and these 18th-century illustrations represent the pinnacle of his craft. Full-color portraits of renowned Japanese samurais pulse with movement, passion, and remarkably fine detail. 112pp. 8⅜ x 11. 0-486-46523-3

ABC OF BALLET, Janet Grosser. Clearly worded, abundantly illustrated little guide defines basic ballet-related terms: arabesque, battement, pas de chat, relevé, sissonne, many others. Pronunciation guide included. Excellent primer. 48pp. 4⁵⁄₁₆ x 5¾.
0-486-40871-X

ACCESSORIES OF DRESS: An Illustrated Encyclopedia, Katherine Lester and Bess Viola Oerke. Illustrations of hats, veils, wigs, cravats, shawls, shoes, gloves, and other accessories enhance an engaging commentary that reveals the humor and charm of the many-sided story of accessorized apparel. 644 figures and 59 plates. 608pp. 6⅛ x 9¼.
0-486-43378-1

ADVENTURES OF HUCKLEBERRY FINN, Mark Twain. Join Huck and Jim as their boyhood adventures along the Mississippi River lead them into a world of excitement, danger, and self-discovery. Humorous narrative, lyrical descriptions of the Mississippi valley, and memorable characters. 224pp. 5⅜ x 8¼. 0-486-28061-6

ALICE STARMORE'S BOOK OF FAIR ISLE KNITTING, Alice Starmore. A noted designer from the region of Scotland's Fair Isle explores the history and techniques of this distinctive, stranded-color knitting style and provides copious illustrated instructions for 14 original knitwear designs. 208pp. 8⅜ x 10⅞. 0-486-47218-3

Browse over 9,000 books at www.doverpublications.com

ALICE'S ADVENTURES IN WONDERLAND, Lewis Carroll. Beloved classic about a little girl lost in a topsy-turvy land and her encounters with the White Rabbit, March Hare, Mad Hatter, Cheshire Cat, and other delightfully improbable characters. 42 illustrations by Sir John Tenniel. 96pp. 5⁵⁄₁₆ x 8¼. 0-486-27543-4

AMERICA'S LIGHTHOUSES: An Illustrated History, Francis Ross Holland. Profusely illustrated fact-filled survey of American lighthouses since 1716. Over 200 stations — East, Gulf, and West coasts, Great Lakes, Hawaii, Alaska, Puerto Rico, the Virgin Islands, and the Mississippi and St. Lawrence Rivers. 240pp. 8 x 10¾.
0-486-25576-X

AN ENCYCLOPEDIA OF THE VIOLIN, Alberto Bachmann. Translated by Frederick H. Martens. Introduction by Eugene Ysaye. First published in 1925, this renowned reference remains unsurpassed as a source of essential information, from construction and evolution to repertoire and technique. Includes a glossary and 73 illustrations. 496pp. 6½ x 9¼. 0-486-46618-3

ANIMALS: 1,419 Copyright-Free Illustrations of Mammals, Birds, Fish, Insects, etc., Selected by Jim Harter. Selected for its visual impact and ease of use, this outstanding collection of wood engravings presents over 1,000 species of animals in extremely lifelike poses. Includes mammals, birds, reptiles, amphibians, fish, insects, and other invertebrates. 284pp. 9 x 12. 0-486-23766-4

THE ANNALS, Tacitus. Translated by Alfred John Church and William Jackson Brodribb. This vital chronicle of Imperial Rome, written by the era's great historian, spans A.D. 14-68 and paints incisive psychological portraits of major figures, from Tiberius to Nero. 416pp. 5⁵⁄₁₆ x 8¼. 0-486-45236-0

ANTIGONE, Sophocles. Filled with passionate speeches and sensitive probing of moral and philosophical issues, this powerful and often-performed Greek drama reveals the grim fate that befalls the children of Oedipus. Footnotes. 64pp. 5⁵⁄₁₆ x 8 ¼. 0-486-27804-2

ART DECO DECORATIVE PATTERNS IN FULL COLOR, Christian Stoll. Reprinted from a rare 1910 portfolio, 160 sensuous and exotic images depict a breathtaking array of florals, geometrics, and abstracts — all elegant in their stark simplicity. 64pp. 8⅜ x 11. 0-486-44862-2

THE ARTHUR RACKHAM TREASURY: 86 Full-Color Illustrations, Arthur Rackham. Selected and Edited by Jeff A. Menges. A stunning treasury of 86 full-page plates span the famed English artist's career, from *Rip Van Winkle* (1905) to masterworks such as *Undine, A Midsummer Night's Dream,* and *Wind in the Willows* (1939). 96pp. 8⅜ x 11.
0-486-44685-9

THE AUTHENTIC GILBERT & SULLIVAN SONGBOOK, W. S. Gilbert and A. S. Sullivan. The most comprehensive collection available, this songbook includes selections from every one of Gilbert and Sullivan's light operas. Ninety-two numbers are presented uncut and unedited, and in their original keys. 410pp. 9 x 12.
0-486-23482-7

THE AWAKENING, Kate Chopin. First published in 1899, this controversial novel of a New Orleans wife's search for love outside a stifling marriage shocked readers. Today, it remains a first-rate narrative with superb characterization. New introductory Note. 128pp. 5⁵⁄₁₆ x 8¼. 0-486-27786-0

BASIC DRAWING, Louis Priscilla. Beginning with perspective, this commonsense manual progresses to the figure in movement, light and shade, anatomy, drapery, composition, trees and landscape, and outdoor sketching. Black-and-white illustrations throughout. 128pp. 8⅜ x 11. 0-486-45815-6

Browse over 9,000 books at www.doverpublications.com

THE BATTLES THAT CHANGED HISTORY, Fletcher Pratt. Historian profiles 16 crucial conflicts, ancient to modern, that changed the course of Western civilization. Gripping accounts of battles led by Alexander the Great, Joan of Arc, Ulysses S. Grant, other commanders. 27 maps. 352pp. 5⅜ x 8½.　　　0-486-41129-X

BEETHOVEN'S LETTERS, Ludwig van Beethoven. Edited by Dr. A. C. Kalischer. Features 457 letters to fellow musicians, friends, greats, patrons, and literary men. Reveals musical thoughts, quirks of personality, insights, and daily events. Includes 15 plates. 410pp. 5⅜ x 8½.　　　0-486-22769-3

BERNICE BOBS HER HAIR AND OTHER STORIES, F. Scott Fitzgerald. This brilliant anthology includes 6 of Fitzgerald's most popular stories: "The Diamond as Big as the Ritz," the title tale, "The Offshore Pirate," "The Ice Palace," "The Jelly Bean," and "May Day." 176pp. 5⅜ x 8½.　　　0-486-47049-0

BESLER'S BOOK OF FLOWERS AND PLANTS: 73 Full-Color Plates from Hortus Eystettensis, 1613, Basilius Besler. Here is a selection of magnificent plates from the *Hortus Eystettensis,* which vividly illustrated and identified the plants, flowers, and trees that thrived in the legendary German garden at Eichstätt. 80pp. 8⅜ x 11.

0-486-46005-3

THE BOOK OF KELLS, Edited by Blanche Cirker. Painstakingly reproduced from a rare facsimile edition, this volume contains full-page decorations, portraits, illustrations, plus a sampling of textual leaves with exquisite calligraphy and ornamentation. 32 full-color illustrations. 32pp. 9⅜ x 12¼.　　　0-486-24345-1

THE BOOK OF THE CROSSBOW: With an Additional Section on Catapults and Other Siege Engines, Ralph Payne-Gallwey. Fascinating study traces history and use of crossbow as military and sporting weapon, from Middle Ages to modern times. Also covers related weapons: balistas, catapults, Turkish bows, more. Over 240 illustrations. 400pp. 7¼ x 10⅛.　　　0-486-28720-3

THE BUNGALOW BOOK: Floor Plans and Photos of 112 Houses, 1910, Henry L. Wilson. Here are 112 of the most popular and economic blueprints of the early 20th century — plus an illustration or photograph of each completed house. A wonderful time capsule that still offers a wealth of valuable insights. 160pp. 8⅜ x 11.

0-486-45104-6

THE CALL OF THE WILD, Jack London. A classic novel of adventure, drawn from London's own experiences as a Klondike adventurer, relating the story of a heroic dog caught in the brutal life of the Alaska Gold Rush. Note. 64pp. 5³⁄₁₆ x 8¼.

0-486-26472-6

CANDIDE, Voltaire. Edited by Francois-Marie Arouet. One of the world's great satires since its first publication in 1759. Witty, caustic skewering of romance, science, philosophy, religion, government — nearly all human ideals and institutions. 112pp. 5³⁄₁₆ x 8¼.　　　0-486-26689-3

CELEBRATED IN THEIR TIME: Photographic Portraits from the George Grantham Bain Collection, Edited by Amy Pastan. With an Introduction by Michael Carlebach. Remarkable portrait gallery features 112 rare images of Albert Einstein, Charlie Chaplin, the Wright Brothers, Henry Ford, and other luminaries from the worlds of politics, art, entertainment, and industry. 128pp. 8⅜ x 11.　　　0-486-46754-6

CHARIOTS FOR APOLLO: The NASA History of Manned Lunar Spacecraft to 1969, Courtney G. Brooks, James M. Grimwood, and Loyd S. Swenson, Jr. This illustrated history by a trio of experts is the definitive reference on the Apollo spacecraft and lunar modules. It traces the vehicles' design, development, and operation in space. More than 100 photographs and illustrations. 576pp. 6¾ x 9¼. 0-486-46756-2

Browse over 9,000 books at www.doverpublications.com

A CHRISTMAS CAROL, Charles Dickens. This engrossing tale relates Ebenezer Scrooge's ghostly journeys through Christmases past, present, and future and his ultimate transformation from a harsh and grasping old miser to a charitable and compassionate human being. 80pp. 5³⁄₁₆ x 8¼.   0-486-26865-9

COMMON SENSE, Thomas Paine. First published in January of 1776, this highly influential landmark document clearly and persuasively argued for American separation from Great Britain and paved the way for the Declaration of Independence. 64pp. 5³⁄₁₆ x 8¼.   0-486-29602-4

THE COMPLETE SHORT STORIES OF OSCAR WILDE, Oscar Wilde. Complete texts of "The Happy Prince and Other Tales," "A House of Pomegranates," "Lord Arthur Savile's Crime and Other Stories," "Poems in Prose," and "The Portrait of Mr. W. H." 208pp. 5³⁄₁₆ x 8¼.   0-486-45216-6

COMPLETE SONNETS, William Shakespeare. Over 150 exquisite poems deal with love, friendship, the tyranny of time, beauty's evanescence, death, and other themes in language of remarkable power, precision, and beauty. Glossary of archaic terms. 80pp. 5³⁄₁₆ x 8¼.   0-486-26686-9

THE COUNT OF MONTE CRISTO: Abridged Edition, Alexandre Dumas. Falsely accused of treason, Edmond Dantès is imprisoned in the bleak Chateau d'If. After a hair-raising escape, he launches an elaborate plot to extract a bitter revenge against those who betrayed him. 448pp. 5³⁄₁₆ x 8¼.   0-486-45643-9

CRAFTSMAN BUNGALOWS: Designs from the Pacific Northwest, Yoho & Merritt. This reprint of a rare catalog, showcasing the charming simplicity and cozy style of Craftsman bungalows, is filled with photos of completed homes, plus floor plans and estimated costs. An indispensable resource for architects, historians, and illustrators. 112pp. 10 x 7.   0-486-46875-5

CRAFTSMAN BUNGALOWS: 59 Homes from "The Craftsman," Edited by Gustav Stickley. Best and most attractive designs from Arts and Crafts Movement publication — 1903–1916 — includes sketches, photographs of homes, floor plans, descriptive text. 128pp. 8¼ x 11.   0-486-25829-7

CRIME AND PUNISHMENT, Fyodor Dostoyevsky. Translated by Constance Garnett. Supreme masterpiece tells the story of Raskolnikov, a student tormented by his own thoughts after he murders an old woman. Overwhelmed by guilt and terror, he confesses and goes to prison. 480pp. 5³⁄₁₆ x 8¼.   0-486-41587-2

THE DECLARATION OF INDEPENDENCE AND OTHER GREAT DOCUMENTS OF AMERICAN HISTORY: 1775-1865, Edited by John Grafton. Thirteen compelling and influential documents: Henry's "Give Me Liberty or Give Me Death," Declaration of Independence, The Constitution, Washington's First Inaugural Address, The Monroe Doctrine, The Emancipation Proclamation, Gettysburg Address, more. 64pp. 5³⁄₁₆ x 8¼.   0-486-41124-9

THE DESERT AND THE SOWN: Travels in Palestine and Syria, Gertrude Bell. "The female Lawrence of Arabia," Gertrude Bell wrote captivating, perceptive accounts of her travels in the Middle East. This intriguing narrative, accompanied by 160 photos, traces her 1905 sojourn in Lebanon, Syria, and Palestine. 368pp. 5⅜ x 8½.
0-486-46876-3

A DOLL'S HOUSE, Henrik Ibsen. Ibsen's best-known play displays his genius for realistic prose drama. An expression of women's rights, the play climaxes when the central character, Nora, rejects a smothering marriage and life in "a doll's house." 80pp. 5³⁄₁₆ x 8¼.   0-486-27062-9

Browse over 9,000 books at www.doverpublications.com

DOOMED SHIPS: Great Ocean Liner Disasters, William H. Miller, Jr. Nearly 200 photographs, many from private collections, highlight tales of some of the vessels whose pleasure cruises ended in catastrophe: the *Morro Castle, Normandie, Andrea Doria, Europa,* and many others. 128pp. 8⅞ x 11¾.   0-486-45366-9

THE DORÉ BIBLE ILLUSTRATIONS, Gustave Doré. Detailed plates from the Bible: the Creation scenes, Adam and Eve, horrifying visions of the Flood, the battle sequences with their monumental crowds, depictions of the life of Jesus, 241 plates in all. 241pp. 9 x 12.   0-486-23004-X

DRAWING DRAPERY FROM HEAD TO TOE, Cliff Young. Expert guidance on how to draw shirts, pants, skirts, gloves, hats, and coats on the human figure, including folds in relation to the body, pull and crush, action folds, creases, more. Over 200 drawings. 48pp. 8¼ x 11.   0-486-45591-2

DUBLINERS, James Joyce. A fine and accessible introduction to the work of one of the 20th century's most influential writers, this collection features 15 tales, including a masterpiece of the short-story genre, "The Dead." 160pp. 5³⁄₁₆ x 8¼.

0-486-26870-5

EASY-TO-MAKE POP-UPS, Joan Irvine. Illustrated by Barbara Reid. Dozens of wonderful ideas for three-dimensional paper fun — from holiday greeting cards with moving parts to a pop-up menagerie. Easy-to-follow, illustrated instructions for more than 30 projects. 299 black-and-white illustrations. 96pp. 8⅜ x 11.

0-486-44622-0

EASY-TO-MAKE STORYBOOK DOLLS: A "Novel" Approach to Cloth Dollmaking, Sherralyn St. Clair. Favorite fictional characters come alive in this unique beginner's dollmaking guide. Includes patterns for Pollyanna, Dorothy from *The Wonderful Wizard of Oz,* Mary of *The Secret Garden,* plus easy-to-follow instructions, 263 black-and-white illustrations, and an 8-page color insert. 112pp. 8¼ x 11. 0-486-47360-0

EINSTEIN'S ESSAYS IN SCIENCE, Albert Einstein. Speeches and essays in accessible, everyday language profile influential physicists such as Niels Bohr and Isaac Newton. They also explore areas of physics to which the author made major contributions. 128pp. 5 x 8.   0-486-47011-3

EL DORADO: Further Adventures of the Scarlet Pimpernel, Baroness Orczy. A popular sequel to *The Scarlet Pimpernel,* this suspenseful story recounts the Pimpernel's attempts to rescue the Dauphin from imprisonment during the French Revolution. An irresistible blend of intrigue, period detail, and vibrant characterizations. 352pp. 5³⁄₁₆ x 8¼.   0-486-44026-5

ELEGANT SMALL HOMES OF THE TWENTIES: 99 Designs from a Competition, Chicago Tribune. Nearly 100 designs for five- and six-room houses feature New England and Southern colonials, Normandy cottages, stately Italianate dwellings, and other fascinating snapshots of American domestic architecture of the 1920s. 112pp. 9 x 12.   0-486-46910-7

THE ELEMENTS OF STYLE: The Original Edition, William Strunk, Jr. This is the book that generations of writers have relied upon for timeless advice on grammar, diction, syntax, and other essentials. In concise terms, it identifies the principal requirements of proper style and common errors. 64pp. 5⅜ x 8½.   0-486-44798-7

THE ELUSIVE PIMPERNEL, Baroness Orczy. Robespierre's revolutionaries find their wicked schemes thwarted by the heroic Pimpernel — Sir Percival Blakeney. In this thrilling sequel, Chauvelin devises a plot to eliminate the Pimpernel and his wife. 272pp. 5³⁄₁₆ x 8¼.   0-486-45464-9

Browse over 9,000 books at www.doverpublications.com